T0196255

PERSPECTIVES
and
POSSIBILITIES

Also by Richard Bellingham

Creating Organizational Soul
Ethical Leadership
Leadership Lexicon
Leadership Myths and Realities
Getting People and Culture Right in Mergers and
Acquisitions
Spiritual Leadership
Corporate Cultural Change
Virtual Teams
HR Optimization
Corporate Culture Change Sourcebook
Intellectual Capital Development
Corporate Wellness Sourcebook
The Complete Guide to Wellness
Designing Effective Health Promotion Programs
Connectedness
The Consciousness Solution
Being at Home in the Universe
The Fables of Boris

PERSPECTIVES
and
POSSIBILITIES
RIFFS AND RANTS OF A VIETNAM
VET TURNED OCTOGENARIAN

Richard Bellingham

PERSPECTIVES AND POSSIBILITIES
Riffs and Rants of a Vietnam Vet turned Octogenarian

iUniverse books may be ordered through booksellers or by contacting:

iUniverse
1663 Liberty Drive
Bloomington, IN 47403
www.iuniverse.com
1-800-Authors (1-800-288-4677)

Because of the dynamic nature of the Internet, any web addresses or links contained in this book may have changed since publication and may no longer be valid. The views expressed in this work are solely those of the author and do not necessarily reflect the views of the publisher, and the publisher hereby disclaims any responsibility for them.

Any people depicted in stock imagery provided by Thinkstock are models, and such images are being used for illustrative purposes only. Certain stock imagery © Thinkstock.

ISBN: 978-1-4917-7110-5 (sc)
ISBN: 978-1-4917-7111-2 (e)

Print information available on the last page.

iUniverse rev. date: 07/15/2015

Dedication

I dedicate this book to Bobbitt - loyal, dependable, steadfast love of my life and wife for 45 years - without whose unwavering support, I would never have been able to do what I do or be who I am.

Contents

Foreword

Here you can jump into the world and inside the head of a man who's been teaching high level execs how to be better managers and people for decades. Glimpse some of how he's done it--by staying chapters and volumes ahead of his students as a voracious devourer of texts and teachings on higher development and related themes.

You'll be treated to highly informed, easy to read, and carefully thought through analyses on dozens of topics. They range from the latest spiritual challenges for people who are post-religious, to what only someone who's been long in the corporate trenches can tell you about leadership, and what organizations private and public ought to be doing, but aren't yet, to make for a better world.

As for taking care of yourself, who better to pick up some pointers from than a 70 year old who thinks nothing of a brisk 10 mile hike in far off places. And who holds his own through 18 holes of golf with much younger men. You can be sure he's read much of what you haven't, because high octane, "get it done" yesterday is just Rick's normal RPM.

Partial disclosure: Rick and I are buddies and have been since after Vietnam. Only in recent years he's volunteered to listen, support, and suggest in all kinds of ways to help me with a mature phase of my life work. Nobody absorbs more, faster, with greater reward for both me as teacher than the way he learns what I've got, the better to help me get it out to others.

Read him and you'll find his youthful, bright, "can do" or what he calls "Mr Possible" spirit infectious. And, for sure, you will have picked up lots of ideas on how and why you, we, and the world can move on for the better.

In this book, he'll update you on numerous current debates, and cutting edge spiritual issues. Here, distilled into a few dozen easily readable, crisp and unusually well informed pieces are digested, crisp essays and intelligent reports by a consummate teacher.

Now for the gold: All of us who are friends know Rick to be a deep, unwaveringly good man, doggedly dedicated to those he loves and the work he considers a calling. Ever humble, in a naturally modest way, for all the mix of mid West, nordic, younger brother with what is compared with most people a super powered ability to step up and maintain the pace at virtually anything he takes on, from physical exercise, to reading, writing, or responding to others.

Every one of these pieces is carefully thought through, like a presentation to a group of execs who've hired Rick to coach. You can tell that whatever the subject, he's done the background reading, and digested the material so that he's made available for you a series of power points, no more than 3 main points per slide.

A philanthropist, lover of humanity, raising his voice first and most volubly, to raise our spirits, as the ultimate comes first, as it truly does now with him and has for most of his lifetime.

But he's been applying these constructs in workaday environments and watching good sense and lots of bad. This book has various neat, organized ways to sort out one from the other and travel paths to a better place.

And whom he's speaking to are those who have, do, and will continue to seek him out and hire him. I sent one of his posts on leadership t to one of the world's foremost exec coaches, Nadine Hack, who helped Nelson Mandela get out of prison, and she raved. Read this book, and so will you.

Introduction

After writing 16 non-best-selling books, my older daughter suggested that I should quit publishing books and start a blog with shorter posts. Why spend all that time writing books that few people read? So I did. In March of 2014, I created my blog www.chigrowsinbrooklyn and wrote my first post. Two years later, I realized I had published about 50 short articles on my blog. The posts weren't exactly going viral, but my steadfast friends were kind enough to read them and respond with helpful suggestions. When I stepped back to take stock of what I had written, I noticed that the posts fell into several broad categories: Spiritual Health, Organizational Health, Leadership, Social Health, and Wellness. Not surprisingly, these categories corresponded to my areas of interest over the past 50 years.

While I took my daughter's advice to start a blog, I am ignoring her advice about publishing another book. So here it is: Perspectives and Possibilities: Riffs and Rants of a Vietnam Vet turned Octogenarian I figured that I should be able to do whatever I want in my eighth decade on this planet. In some ways, this book is like blended whiskey.

It is a highly distilled version of multiple ingredients – in this case, all the books I've written + 50 years of studying these topic areas. In other ways, it is like a fine wine – the ideas have aged well with time. As I get older, the ideas become more refined. So, the title of the book reflects my best intentions. It shares perspectives and possibilities for living a meaningful life in the face of relentless challenges.

And, yes, it contains the riffs and rants of a Vietnam Vet. When I was in Vietnam I saw suffering I never wanted to see. I heard screams I never wanted to hear, I felt fear I never wanted to feel.

With grace and luck, I made it back safely –only emotionally wounded and spiritually scarred. Since that time, with effort and luck, I have seen wonderful places I never imagined seeing, I have heard baby coos that I never would have believed could sound so good, and I have opened to a love and grace that I had never thought possible.

So this book is for sharing where I've come in my improbable transformation from a writhing veteran, scared of probabilities, to an inveterate writer, fearless of possibilities.

I can only hope that these perspectives open you to new possibilities.

Spiritual Health

This chapter reflects the dominant interest in my life. There are 20 posts in the chapter compared with less than 10 in each of the other chapters. While I made my living in the areas covered in the other chapters, I made my life in this chapter.

As you will see when you read this chapter, these posts emerged from multiple sources: theoretical physics, neuroscience, esoteric psychology, philosophy, theology, and eastern mysticism. What strikes me, as I edit these posts to flow in a book format, is the realization that all of these ideas boil down to some fairly simple principles: love, share, care, let go, open-up, let in, connect, and dance. It's all about finding the music that moves your soul and spontaneously expressing yourself through a joyful dance with life.

Spiritual Awakening

On March 10, 2015, I joined 40,000 spiritual seekers in an on-line Master Class on "The Next Level of Spiritual Awakening" with Ken Wilber. He discussed the differences between spirituality and religion, the differences in hierarchies, and four frameworks for spiritual growth. During this 90 minute session, he provided conceptual constructs for growing up, showing up, waking up, and cleaning up. In this post, I would like to honor his contribution to spiritual development and share some tidbits I've picked up along my path related to those areas.

Ken Wilber was born in Oklahoma City in 1949. In 1967, he enrolled as a pre-med student at Duke University. He became inspired by Eastern literature, particularly the Tao Te Ching. In 1973, Wilber completed his first book, *The Spectrum of Consciousness*, in which he sought to integrate knowledge from disparate fields. In 1982, he published the *Holographic Paradigm and Other Paradoxes*, which explored the ways in which holography relates to the fields of consciousness, mysticism, and science. Since that time, he has published over 25 books on Integral Psychology and Unity Consciousness. His work has been published in 30 languages. Clearly, Wilber has made an enormous contribution to the integration of multiple points of view and has demonstrated the interdependence among them. His work clearly deserves the honors and recognition it has received.

Since I have written extensively about the differences between religion and spirituality in other posts and in several books, I will not bore you with further pontification on that subject. Although Wilber articulates those differences more powerfully than I do, our views are similar.

I find Wilber's simple construct on hierarchies very helpful. He discusses the differences between dominating hierarchies and growth hierarchies. In dominant hierarchies, people move up whatever ladder they are climbing in order to establish powerful positioning and to exploit and exclude the people they "rise above." In growth hierarchies, the motivation for moving up the scales is to elevate your level of functioning and development so that you can include and help others. People who are attracted to dominant hierarchies tend to push people down. People who are attracted to growth hierarchies tend to lift people up. The spiritual implications are obvious.

In the master class, I particularly enjoyed the frameworks Wilber discussed on growing up, showing up, waking up, and cleaning up. Since I have a bias for 5 point scales, I have taken some liberty to modify his scales in the following grid. Below the grid, I offer explanations of the development levels and the corresponding scales.

Levels of Development	Growing Up	Showing Up	Waking Up	Cleaning Up
Cosmic or Being Centric	Integral Thinking	THIS* (Cosmic being orientation)	Unified	Applying
World Centric	Inclusive Thinking	We (Collective, Cultural Orientation)	Conscious	Dealing
Tribal Centric	Rational Thinking	You (Mutual relationship orientation)	Awake	Leaving in the Unconscious
Ethno-Centric	Mythical Thinking	I (Interior, intentional orientation)	Dreaming	Repressing
Ego Centric	Magical Thinking	It (Exterior, behavioral orientation)	Asleep	Disowning

*see www.energysway.com

Growing Up: The scale on growing up represents different levels of thinking at the various levels of development. If you are ego centric or narcissistic, you will likely engage in magical thinking which simply means that you will expect events to occur because you wish them to be so. It's solipsism in all it's glory. If you are ethno-centric, you will likely engage in mythical thinking, which means accepting all the beliefs and legends associated with your race. It's racial politics at its finest. If you are tribal-centric, you will, at best, engage in rational thinking, which means you will be looking for ways to advance your religion or nation independent of

5

ideology or dogma. It's patriotism at its best. If you are world-centric, you are more likely to engage in inclusive thinking which means looking out for what's best for the environment and the global economy. It's progressivism with a peaceful and productive purpose. If you are cosmic or being centric, you are likely to engage in integral thinking which means understanding the inter-relationships of multi-dimensional systems. It's interdependence with light, love, and power. As we grow up, we move through these phases and up this scale. Moving up and through is not dependent on age. There are many old people who are stuck in magical, mythical, or tribal thinking; and there are many young people who have already advanced to inclusive and integral thinking. If you are interested in further elaboration, Robert Carkhuff, Ph.D. has done an enormous amount of work on growth scales and on interdependent thinking.

Showing Up: The scale on showing up represents differences in orientation at the various levels of development. The simple question is, "how do you show up?" If you "show up" with a selfish and external orientation, you are probably most concerned with the "it" of life, e.g. money, power, status, achievement, educational degree etc. If you "show up" with an internal and intentional orientation, you are probably most concerned with the "I" of life, e.g. your feelings, thoughts, sensations, values, etc. If you "show up" with a relationship orientation, you are probably most concerned with the "you" of life, e.g. your spouse, partners, friends, children, customers, etc. You will likely be looking for mutually supportive and beneficial relationships. If you "show up" with a collective, cultural orientation, you are probably most concerned about the "we" of life, e.g. the norms, values, support systems of the groups in which you participate. If you "show up" with a cosmic being orientation, you are probably most concerned with the THIS of life, e.g. the experiences and transformational events that lead you and your loved ones to feel more at One with the Universe. We can "show up" differently in our lives depending upon the situation in which we find ourselves and on the capabilities we have developed over time. Artie Egendorf, Ph.D., in his soon to be published book, *Spiritual Superfood*, provides concrete ways to show up differently in our lives.

Waking Up: The scale on waking up represents differences in our levels of spiritual awareness. Clearly, if you go through life in a sleeping state, there is virtually no awareness. If you spend most of your life dreaming, then there will probably be few moments of alert, focused awareness. If you are awake most of the time, then you will be much more aware of your thoughts, feelings, and sensations. If you have been able to develop a conscious "impartial observer" or "witness" in your life, then you will not only increase awareness, but you will also be able to objectively notice the thoughts, feelings, and sensations that pass through your consciousness and be able to notice them, acknowledge them, and move on/let them go. If you have a unity consciousness, then you will always be looking for ways to align your energy centers and bring things together in interdependent ways. The Russian philosopher and spiritual teacher of the early to mid-20th century, G. I. Gurdjieff, taught that most humans live their lives in a state of hypnotic "waking sleep", but that it is possible to transcend to a higher state of consciousness and achieve full human potential. Gurdjieff developed a method for doing so, calling his discipline "The Work."

Gurdjieff's notion of humans having the potential to develop a crystallized "I" is similar to Wilber's idea of "the witness."

Cleaning Up. Unfortunately, it is practically impossible to grow up, show up, and wake up without "cleaning up" along the way. What Wilber means by cleaning up is to go down and in before coming up and out, i.e. it's very hard to go forward without going backward first. In order to develop higher levels of consciousness, we need to confront our lower levels of neuroticism. As Dr. Egendorf would say, we need to turn toward, tune in, read, and care before we can grow and bloom. At level 1 in this scale, we disown our early trauma and deny our neurotic manifestations. At level 2, we repress memories that cause us grief and discomfort. At level 3, we prefer to leave traumatic experiences in our unconscious and hope their ugly heads don't keep re-appearing. At level 4, we deal with all of life's experiences for better or for worse and learn from them. At level 5, we leverage the experiences by using what we learned from working through them and applying them to all areas of our lives.

In this post, I have tried to summarize and re-frame a vast body of work that Ken Wilber has contributed to the literature and to our spiritual awakening. Even though this post is a much reduced and re-framed version of the messages he delivered in his on-line master class, what strikes me is the power of the simple accessible phrases: grow up, show up, wake up, and clean up. Each of us can assign our own meaning to those four action suggestions. And hopefully, each of us will be able to apply those messages to our own lives and to the lives of others. Thank you, Ken Wilber, for your provocative and profound contributions.

Conscious Dualism
Making the higher active
and the lower passive

Dualism means the tendency of humans to perceive and understand the world as being divided into two discreet categories. Dualism exists in many belief systems including Zoroastrianism, Christianity, Taoism and Confucianism. In these beliefs the universe is divided into the complementary oppositions, e.g. good and evil. In traditions such as classical Hinduism, Zen Buddhism or Islamic Sufism, a key to enlightenment is "transcending" this sort of dualistic thinking.

In Chinese philosophy, the opposition and combination of the universe's two basic principles of yin and yang play a large role and are important features of Taoism, both as a philosophy and as a religion. Yin and yang are used to describe how opposite or contrary forces are interconnected and interdependent in the natural world; and, how they give rise to each other as they interrelate to one another. Many natural dualities (such as light and dark, high and low, hot and cold, fire and water, life and death, and so on) are thought of as physical manifestations of the yin-yang concept. The concept is also a central principle in different forms of Chinese martial arts and exercise, such as qigong. Yin and yang can be thought of as complementary forces interacting to form a dynamic system in which the whole is greater than the parts. Everything has both yin and yang aspects, (for instance shadow cannot exist without light). Yin or yang manifest more or less strongly in every person.

Some of the common associations with yang and yin, respectively, are: male and female, active and passive, motion and stillness. The yin and yang symbol in actuality has very little to do with Western dualism; instead it represents the philosophy of balance, where two opposites co-exist in harmony and are able to transmute into each other. In the yin-yang symbol there is a dot of yin in yang and a dot of yang in yin. This symbolizes the inter-connectedness of the opposite forces as different aspects of Tao. Contrast is needed to create a distinguishable reality, without which we would experience nothingness, i.e. you need friction for fire. Therefore, the independent principles of yin and yang are actually dependent on one another for each other's distinguishable existence. An underlying principle in Taoism states that within every independent entity lies a part of its opposite. Within sickness lies health and vice versa. This is because all opposites are manifestations of the single Tao, and are therefore not independent from one another, but rather a variation of the same unifying force throughout all of nature.

For me, conscious dualism is the awareness of two different forces constantly working within us – the higher and the lower. It is the ability to observe how the higher self and the lower self manifest themselves in our lives and to increase our intentionality for making the higher active and the lower passive and, ultimately, to transcend both of them.

In my experience, our higher self reveals itself through, acceptance, forgiveness, and compassion. We need to accept the fact that everyone is struggling with their own issues and most of us are doing our best to care for ourselves and for others. We need to accept our own limitations and the limitations of people in our lives, but not let those limitations limit us. We need to forgive others for whatever offenses they may have caused us and hope others will forgive us for our own transgressions, shortcomings, hateful acts, and sins of omission. Finally, we need to find compassion in our hearts for all living creatures on our common planet. These words are all easy to say, but I find it is all too easy to slip into my lower self.

Our lower self shows itself through imagination, identification, and negative emotion. Imagination is our tendency to exaggerate our own self importance and centrality. It is fed by our egos (well-fed, I might say) and results in highly inflated opinions of our capabilities, power, and presence. As a friend of mine would say, "we are often prone to inhaling our own PR." I am often guilty of having more confidence than my capabilities would suggest is appropriate. And this confidence easily spills over into arrogance.

Identification is our tendency to get over-invested in any given image, role, position, religion, nation, or ideology. The belief system usually associated with that identification causes us to draw conclusions and act in ways that are not always in our own best interest and certainly don't advance our growth and development as evolved human beings. I am guilty of identifying as a psychologist, an outsider, a provocateur, an athlete, or a parent. I don't particularly identify with any nation, or religion, but I have many other identifies I can hide behind.

Negative emotions are those feelings that sink us into depression, rage, disorientation or any other energy depleting states. They are spiritual anchors. I am guilty of reacting for the slightest reason with impatience, irritation, intolerance, and disgust. While I'm much quicker to observe these emotions and let them go, they continue to raise their ugly heads in my ever-vulnerable psyche.

It seems to me that the goal is to make our higher selves active and our lower selves passive. The real questions are:

1.   Can I be more conscious of how and when my lower and higher selves show up?
2.   Can I be more intentional about connecting to my higher self and make an effort to activate it?
3.   Can I transcend my dualistic nature and find joy in those "enlightened moments?"

Yes, consciousness, intentionality, and transcendence seem to be the most useful ways to deal constructively with our dualistic nature.

Finding Meaning
In the middle or at the margins

"The human race is a monotonous affair. Most people spend the greatest part of their time working in order to live, and what little freedom remains so fills them with fear that they seek out any and every means to be rid of it."

Johann Wolfgang von Goethe, *The Sorrows of Young Werther*

Goethe describes well the experience of people who are trying to find meaning while living in the middle. People either feel bored because each day looks pretty much the same, or they feel terrified because they don't know how to fill the void freedom presents or face the void death presents.

Let's start with what I mean by "the middle." Technically, it means living within 2 standard deviations of the mean under the bell curve – a life that is largely similar to 95% of the population. Practically, it means a conventional life that probably entails a 9-5 job (or 8-6 or 7-7 or 11-11) with a recognizable and predictable career path – lots of safety, security, and relative certainty.

Living at the margins means leading an unconventional life that usually results in feeling like an outsider. People living at the margins have to get comfortable with a lack of safety, security, and certainty. They are typically ignored, rejected, maligned, or killed because their ideas threaten the status quo or traditional beliefs. These rare people are the ones who question authority, challenge assumptions, and mercilessly destroy strongly held beliefs about the world and about humankind. They are also the ones that create disruptive change for better or for worse.

I am not suggesting that finding meaning is impossible in the middle. I'm just saying that the pull toward "normalcy" is stronger there. No matter where we live – in the middle or at the margins – it is still our sole responsibility to find meaning – it is not pre-determined. Victor Frankl, the author of Man's Search for Meaning, challenges us to always look for possibilities against the backdrop of reality. If Victor Frankl can say that as a holocaust survivor, our trivial excuses for giving up the search are pretty pathetic.

If we are living in the middle, we need to come to grips with these **risk factors for a meaningful life:**

- <u>Beliefs:</u> Religious belief systems encourage us to give up our individual identify for the identity of the collective. The same is true of political ideology or nationalism.
- <u>Language:</u> We are bombarded with words to describe reality, when the universe does not require pedantic explanation. Wittgenstein understood this best when he exposed the limits of language to describe any esoteric experience.
- <u>Expectations</u>: We think the universe should conform to our expectations, when it is under no obligation to do so. The formula for unhappiness is to hold onto expectations that have no connection to reality. Seeking possibilities and holding onto expectations are two different phenomena.

- <u>Culture</u>: Civilization is littered with 6,000 years of myth, superstition, and dogma. The norms and values that shape our beliefs and behaviors exert a strong influence on how we find meaning.
- <u>Rules:</u> Playing by the rules increases our comfort zone, but comfort and growth don't co-exist. Rules, though necessary for an orderly world, tend to restrict us to an ordinary life. Restrictions limit what may be possible in our lives. Its like trying to create a symphony on one scale of the piano or only being able to color within the lines.

If we are living in the middle or at the margins, we need to reflect on these questions:

- How do I seek knowledge without prejudice and see my path as a journey? Finding meaning may mean suspending judgments and opening to ideas I never considered before. Staying open to possibilities.
- How do I focus on soul first and personality second? Meaning is rarely found in appearance, personality, or material possession. It is found in the essence. It's staying committed to the spirit instead of the letter.
- How do I stay open to feelings? There is more richness and depth in feelings than in intellectual constructs. We can't intellectualize our way to meaning. In fact, our thoughts can be the biggest barrier to getting at something higher and deeper.
- How do I find meaning when bad things happen for no apparent reason? Contrary to pithy reassurances and vacuous sentimentality, there isn't a reason for everything. Sometimes, we have to dig hard for meaning.

- How do I keep ever-present the perspective that life is limited and precious? Our mortality needs to sit on our shoulder and whisper in our ear: Now! Now!
- How do I find joy? Where do I find joy? What's keeping me from being more joyful? These are the questions that will move us to do more, see more, and be more.

Meaning is measured in moments. The top 5% of earners may possess 70% of the wealth, but they don't have a claim on meaning. And I strongly suspect that those 5 percent folks may be missing out on what is profoundly important and meaningful in life. When my 2 year old grand-daughter falls asleep on my chest for an hour, that is a moment to be treasured, not an hour lost to pile up more money.

The challenge of living in the middle is to avoid getting caught in the flow, whatever that flow may be. It could be workaholism, alcoholism, militarism, or materialism. It doesn't really matter. It's just another "ism" to put us to sleep and to lose track of what's most meaningful.

The challenge of living in the margins is to sustain the courage, commitment, and confidence it requires to continue the search. It's lonely on the margins and you are more likely to be punished for a different path than rewarded and celebrated for it. It's scary on the margins and you are always going to feel pressure to pull back and find every means, as Goethe says, to get rid of it. Fear chases freedom. The question is, can we welcome it instead of run away from it?

I believe we are more likely to find meaning at the margins than in the middle. It's not the safest path, but it's the one that will provide enough shocks to our system that we might wake up and dig deeper. Clearly, there are multiple ways to find meaning in the middle. I just believe that safety can be hazardous to your health because of the risk factors I discussed above. Whether you are searching for meaning from the margins or the middle, the questions and risk factors still apply. Happy searching.

Free Will . . . . . or Not

Copernicus destroyed the myth that we are central. Darwin destroyed the myth that we are special. Now, Crick and the neuroscientists want to destroy the myth that we are conscious. They suggest that all behaviors are simply manifestations of a conditioned brain – when the brain dies, we die. They posit that we operate simply out of habit. Essentially, they conclude that we are automatons with no free choice. Quite simply, our brain sends out zombie agents to control our behavior. Depressed yet? You may not need to be.

While I accept the fact that we are not central and we are not as special as we would like to think we are, I believe that free will varies by level of functioning. In short, low functioning people do not operate with consciousness and intentionality and thus have no free will. High functioning people do operate consciously and intentionally and thus can have moments of free will.

Level of functioning depends on how well we think, relate, and plan. And free will can be measured by our level of consciousness. The chart below summarizes my point of view:

Functioning	Planning	Thinking	Relating	Consciousness
Leader	S-EP-R	3D Rotated	Interdependent	Enlightened Service
Contributor	S-OP-R	3D Nested	Collaborative	Harmonious Inclusion
Participant	S-P-R	3D	Independent	Logical Analysis
Observer	S-O-R	2D	Competitive	Informed Choice
Detractor	S-R	1D	Dependent	Automatic Habit

Note: The first four scales were developed by Robert Carkhuff.

Functioning: Level of functioning describes how we act in the world at any point in time. The five levels are leader, contributor, participant, observer, and detractor. In any given moment, we may operate at any one of these levels. Sometimes, we are detractors. At other times, we are observers. Hopefully, in critical moments, we step up and assume a leadership role. The questions to consider are how often do we operate in each role and to what extent are we making the right choices regarding what role a situation requires.

Planning: Our ability to plan depends on how well we process information. S-R means stimulus-response. We simply react automatically to any situation that we confront. There is no free will at this level. We may as well be one of Pavlov's dogs. Our brains simply form habits based on experience, culture, and genetic-pre-disposition. There is no "I." S-O-R means there is an organism between the stimulus and response that makes choices on how to act. Those choices depend on the response repertoire that the person has developed over time to deal with situations. The range of choices may be limited or robust depending again on culture, experience, and heredity. A neuroscientist could still claim that the quality of responses is entirely dependent on the brain and its neurological connections. S-P-R means there is someone processing all the choices available and exercising some free will on the best course of action. Here is where the game changes. At this level, there is an "I" who is looking for personal meaning in the range of choices available. S-OP-R means that the person has shifted from "I" to "We." The person is seeking organizational connections and is looking out for the well-being of the community. At this level of functioning, the person is actively seeking ways to be helpful to a larger whole. S-EP-R means that the person is concerned about the environment as well as others and is processing information contextually so that the full implications of choices can be considered. The exercise of free will grows larger as one moves up the scale. It is less determined by stimuli and conditioning.

Thinking: Each level of planning requires a different level of thinking. For S-R functioning, the thinking is one-dimensional. S-O-R functioning requires two-dimensional thinking. A person needs to see relationships. S-P-R functioning requires three-dimensional thinking. The person needs to understand the components, functions, and processes involved in a system in order to be effective. S-OP-R functioning not only requires 3D thinking, but it also needs to take into account the conditions in which actions are nested. S-EP-R functioning has the added requirement of specifying standards for each choice and being able to rotate all dimensions based on changing conditions and standards. Free will takes on new meaning as one moves up the scale.

Relating: Each level of thinking requires a different way of relating. One-dimensional people are dependent on someone else giving them a stimulus to react to. Two-dimensional people tend to think of every situation as win or lose and thus relate competitively. Three-dimensional thinkers consider multiple factors in their processing, but are inclined to relate independently. They are likely to participate fully but not contribute to others. People who nest every stimulus in the conditions in which it occurs, are more likely to collaborate with others. They see the larger picture and are open to sharing ways to be helpful. People who can rotate all dimensions to achieve higher levels of excellence relate interdependently. They actively seek ways to serve others and to achieve an aspirational and inspirational vision. Relating interdependently with others to accomplish a higher purpose requires consciousness and intentionality – the two fundamental ingredients of free will.

Consciousness: Free will can be measured by level of consciousness. At level 1, people are reacting habitually with conditioned responses. At level 2, people are making discriminations and choices about preferred courses of action, but free will is limited to the range of options within their repertoire. At level 3, people are logically sorting through multiple sources of data to arrive at new ideas. This is the beginning of free will. At level 4, people are finely tuned in to the culture and conditions in which they are living, learning, and working and are creating harmonious solutions to benefit the common good. At level 5, people are continuously generating innovative ways to achieve higher standards in service of humanity in general. This type of enlightened service optimizes free will.

In summary, free will is the ability to make <u>choices</u> unimpeded and undetermined by certain factors such as physical constraints, social constraints and mental constraints e.g. compulsions phobias, neurological disorders, or genetic predispositions. The principle of free will has religious, legal, ethical, and scientific implications, e.g. neuro-scientific findings regarding free will may suggest different ways of predicting human behavior.

Though it is a commonly-held intuition that we have free will, it has been widely debated throughout history not only whether that is true, but even how to define the concept of free will. How exactly must the will be free, what exactly must the will be free from, in order for us to have free will?

This post suggests that free will needs to considered according to level of functioning. As such, it complicates matters for the scientific reductionists who tend to see everything through the lens of physical materialism, i.e. it's all about the brain – there is no consciousness and thus no free will. I hope this post introduces another lens through which we may be able freely and willfully to exam the dimensions of free will. I guess I'm just not willing to let go of this last myth that we humans cling to.

Possibility

As the world veers ever more perilously toward the precipice, it doesn't seem like a giant leap to suggest that we need a major shift in thinking and relating. Essentially, we need to start thinking about ourselves as connected vs. separate and we need to start relating to each other interdependently vs. competitively. This post will address the possibilities of making that shift and the planetary potential if we can make it happen. I will first define what possibility and potential mean and then share the results of recent scientific research that substantiates wisdom philosophies from the ancient past. I will conclude with some implications for each of us in making that shift.

Possibility can be defined as the chance that something might exist, happen, or be true. Possibilities represent the qualities that could make someone or something better in the future, i.e. the capabilities and capacity to become or develop that may lead to future success.

Potential can be defined as capable of development into actuality.

So the question is, what is the possibility that we have the potential to see ourselves as connected and interdependent, i.e. what is the chance that an idea could become an actuality? In this case, what is the chance that we can think of ourselves as interconnected and thus relate interdependently to actualize potential on this planet?

Let me set the stage with the science. According to new scientific research, all matter and we our-selves consist of forms of light. In his book *Vibrational Medicine,* physician Richard Gerber describes **all matter as "frozen light,"** light which has been slowed down and become solid. A quantum physicist would say that light in this context does not slow down-it always moves at the speed of light. Rather the light's photons get absorbed; its energy has been transferred. Gerber points out that atoms are primarily empty space. What fills them, he says, are packets of light that sometimes act as matter.

If our bodies, at least metaphorically, are made of frozen light, they maintain the characteristics of light, which means they have frequency. Matter then may be thought of as light of a higher density. Thus, drawing on the implications of modern physics, we can conclude that human beings are made of light held in matter.

It is important to stress that Gerber's concept of matter as frozen light may not be merely metaphoric. Gerber describes the cellular matrix of the physical body as a complex energy interference pattern, interpenetrated by the organizing bio energetic field of the etheric body. The physical body is therefore an energy field, and the field is made up of segments of vibration. As physicist Max Planck determined, higher frequency light means higher energy light. This concept also applies to what we think of as matter because we now know that all matter, not just quantum matter, also has frequency and thus waves-another scientific revelation that has radically changed the way we see the physical world. Using simple equations, Louis De Broglie discovered the wavelengths of waves that correspond to matter, which are not visible to us. Breakthroughs in quantum physics imply that all matter, including matter that makes up the human body, is itself made up of waves of light. It is therefore interesting to note that many ancient teachings saw humans as engendered by light, as children of light.

The Nobel Prize winning physicist David Bohm has written about what he calls the implicate order of the holographic universe. This concept suggests that the entire universe is an ever-changing cosmic hologram that is layered with information. Each layer holds a higher order of information and each higher order is enfolded in an aspect of space/time. The higher order may be thought of as consciousness that filters wave-like into form. Because it is a hologram, every segment contains information about the entire universe. Thus, consciousness is indeed in all things. Light is both the medium and the message.

Moreover, Bohm's work in quantum physics suggests that at the subatomic level all points in space are essentially the same, and therefore nothing is actually separate from anything else. This property is called non-locality. Bell's Theorem, developed a few years later by J. S. Bell, a Swiss physicist, provided mathematical proof of non-locality. If we think about locality in terms of the particle behavior of light (a specific point in space), then non-locality can be seen in terms of light behaving as a wave (indistinguishable and interconnected).

What these concepts tell us is that, at the heart of our universe, there are no separate parts to anything, and that everything is connected to everything else. Moreover, they explain how information can be transferred superluminously, or faster than the speed of light. For example, if two photons are non-locally connected, communication between them can be instantaneous because they are not truly separate.

These discoveries from quantum physics have important implications for the evolution of human consciousness predicted by the Andean prophecies. As Bohm states, the world is an "unbroken wholeness"; everything is non-locally interconnected. We need to learn to perceive holistically because our world and the entire universe is actually interconnected. It is erroneous to continue to perceive our world as a conglomeration of separate, unrelated parts. In light of emergent scientific principles, the old view of reality is decidedly misleading.

This holistic way of perceiving the world mirrors the teachings of ancient people such as the Inca. Buddhist and Hindu teachings have also long told us that everything is energy dancing in form, and that the dance is a continuous weaving of the form and the formless. Now research from the frontiers of science is telling us the same thing.

Given this level of interconnectedness, wouldn't it make sense to start relating to each other interdependently, i.e. actively seeking ways to help each other succeed instead of striving to defeat and dominate each other.

In *The Last Particle in the Universe*, a recent (2012) book, Sean Carroll, a theoretical physicist at the California Institute of Technology, explains the science of interconnectedness. After receiving his doctorate from Harvard, he pursued research on particle physics, cosmology, and gravitation.

He concludes in the book that we are all interconnected and interdependent.

Isn't it strange that ideas proposed over 2,600 years ago, which have been categorically dismissed by scientists, are now being substantiated by scientists?

So what's the possibility of achieving the planetary potential that awaits our awakening. It's a very real possibility if only we can shift our view of the world from "I am separate and central" to "We are connected and interdependent."

Freedom

It's a terrible feeling and a freeing experience to have your illusions destroyed.

As I walked down the streets of Saigon and watched the army trucks full of terrified, tough kids purposely drive through mud puddles so that they could laugh gleefully as the brown, polluted water splashed randomly on the elegant, white, long dresses of the beautiful Vietnamese women, I knew my view of the world had been irrevocably shaken. In the name of freedom, we denied the Vietnamese their right to freely choose who they would be and how they would live.

Were these mud-splashing kids evil? No. They were unwitting victims of a systematic campaign to dehumanize a nation of people they knew nothing about. No, they knew nothing about the long history of a long appendage of Southern China who had resisted the Chinese, thrown out the French, and would now out-last the mighty Americans. They knew nothing about the individual lives and aspirations of this largely Buddhist nation who was trying to scrape out a living and find some meaning in a relentlessly demanding life. They were duped to believe in an illusion that America was there to spread freedom in the world.

Freedom is typically defined as the state of not being imprisoned or enslaved. It is defined in the negative. There are many tangible ways to be in prison and slavery is the worst of evils, but there are intangible ways to be imprisoned or enslaved as well, perhaps the greatest of which is to be trapped in our illusions.

Alan Schwartz, a long time instructor at the Gestalt Institute and Esalen, says "our greatest delusion is to think we are not crazy!" Destroying that illusion is one of the most freeing acts we can take. Gurdjieff's mission was to "mercilessly destroy the beliefs we have about ourselves and the world. So here's a freeing truth. The world is crazy and we are crazy. We all have demons or saboteurs or dark sides whether they are named or not, and whether we are even aware of them or not. The quantity and quality of the sages and saboteurs in our psyche may vary, but none of us is entirely sane.

In my view, if we want to be truly free we need to free ourselves from the intangible prisons of our mind and to make more effort in our lives to create think, relate, love and serve in more innovative ways.

Specifically, we need to free ourselves from:

- the tyranny of normalcy
- the illusion of security
- the fighting mind
- the acquisitive mind
- the tribal mind
- external controls and restraints
- the prisons of our mind
- the ideological mind

And we need to make conscious effort to free ourselves to:

- actualize our own changeable destinies
- generate new responses to changing conditions
- love
- think
- develop a soul
- serve

In the song, *Me and Bobby McGee*, Janis Joplin sang, "freedom is just another word for having nothing less to lose." When the inmates I served in a jail rehabilitation would quote that phrase, I would reply, "Freedom is also having no choice because your values are so clear." "You feel trapped because you don't know who you want to be and you want to be more in control of your life." In my view, we can be trapped in so many ways. The only way out is to know who we are, what we want, and then create the responses required to feel more free. Perhaps a place to start is to confront the illusions we have about ourselves and about the world.

How and Why

We hear a lot of either/or options in our lives. Either you can do this or you can do that. And how often is an acknowledgement of a different point of view accompanied, by a "but . . . . . ?" Ya, but I think . . . . . ! This post addresses the need to see the complementarity of differences and the need to ask "how" AND "why." As the eastern philosophers would say, "there is a yin in every yang, and a yang in every yin." Both need each other.

In a simple and profound way, Carkhuff suggests that there are two dimensions to human behavior, responsive and initiative. One without the other is crazy. While it is a wonderful trait to be responsive and supportive, there are times we need to be initiative and directive. Think parenting. All "ask" and no "tell" will lead to chaos. All "tell" and no "ask" will result in squashing creativity at a minimum and alienation at a maximum.

Limiting ourselves to one side or the other creates polarization and divisiveness. Think politics. The republicans and democrats are locked in. As a result, we have a gridlocked system. I would like to explore the notion of complementary and how it can lead to a greater sense of interconnectedness and interdependence. New discoveries in theoretical physics support this idea.

The basic questions of how and why demonstrate this point. Scientists prefer to invest all their energy in "how" the universe works. More spiritually oriented people prefer to ponder "why" there is something vs. nothing, i.e. why am I here?

Politicians focus primarily on "how" they are going to raise enough money and secure enough votes to get "elected." In the process, they lose track of "why" they want to get elected in the first place. Presumably, the reason is to achieve a position of power to be able to make things better for all the people – not just the people who fund their campaigns.

Religious institutions concentrate on finding new members, building bigger churches, and making their budgets, i.e. how to grow. In the process, they lose track of the goal of living in the question "why" do I exist – what is my purpose in life? I don't presume to suggest there are any definitive answers, but we should at least live in the question.

Even athletes are vulnerable to becoming compulsively obsessed with "how" to win a game and reaching the top of their field instead of pausing to ask "why" am I devoting all my energy to this singular pursuit.

What a difference it would make if scientists, politicians, athletes, and preachers complemented their "how" questions with "why" questions. What a difference it would make if mystics, critics, and couch potatoes complemented their "why" questions with "how" questions.

Just as responsiveness increases the potency of initiative and vice versa, asking "how" complements the "why" and "why" strengthens the "how." This phenomenon even works in educational evaluation. How much rigor should go into the evaluation process and what is the meaning derived (why are we doing this?). The current emphasis on evaluating teachers and student performance has not had a big effect on educational outcomes, but has served to drive teachers out of the profession. We know that educational success comes from treating teachers with respect and paying them accordingly. Why would we think that treating teachers like losers and not paying them competitive wages would attract excellent candidates into the field? AND how can we do a better job of attracting, developing, and retaining the most talented and capable people into education.

We are living in a polarized and divided world. All of the examples above are simply manifestations of our one-sided, narrow, and limited thinking. We see and define ourselves by our differences instead of our similarities. When we spend all of our time, money, and resources trying to figure out "how" to defeat or eliminate those who are different, we miss the larger point of "why" we are here in the first place.

Modern humans have only been on the earth a small fraction of its existence – 200,000 years of its 4,000,000,000 life (1/20,000). That's a flash. The big questions are "how" do we become something other than a bug on the windshield of history AND "why" have we had this unique opportunity and gift to develop and grow like no other species? If we lived in those questions, perhaps we would feel more grateful for every moment we have, and we would act with more grace and compassion toward all our fellow species. Ask how AND why.

Making Love

Don't get excited. This is not a sex post or an intercourse guide. Although I am a fan of great sex, this post deals with making love to life – in simple, everyday ways that don't require expensive props or bundles of money. It's simply an attitude and a choice.

I should preface this post by saying that I was a participant in the "Make Love, Not War" movement in the 60s. During my year of military service in Vietnam, I was directly confronted with the evils of war. I joined 500,000 candle-burning protesters in a march on Washington wearing my uniform. I subsequently joined Vietnam Veterans against the war. Since I physically left Vietnam 45 years ago, I have continued to carry the inspiring experiences and devastating trauma with me emotionally, intellectually, and spiritually. What I have observed, since participating in a military war of aggression, is that we are fighting different kinds of wars all the time. We are at war with ourselves, our teachers, our bosses, our co-workers, our spouses, our children . . . . even our own mortality.

For me, choosing to make love instead of war is a daunting challenge. In addition to carrying some scars from my war experience, I also struggle with personality characteristics that invite my private wars to constantly raise their ugly heads. I tend to be impatient, intolerant, and driven. Instead of patiently, gently, and sensitively finding solutions to problems, I try to force my way through. So I am writing this post not as a model of peace and tranquility, but as someone who has learned through great effort and brilliant teachers that there are many wonderful ways to make love and few good ways to make war.

Yes, there is more than one way to make love. Its about lightening up, being playful, letting go of things we can't change, letting in the joy of life, opening up to spontaneous experience, dancing in stillness or in silliness, being fully present in the moment. Making love to life doesn't mean ignoring difficulties, avoiding problems, sticking your head in the sand, or denying realities. It means rejoicing in the day we have been given and dancing with the demons we have acquired through one source or another.

Here are some possibilities for making love you may want to consider.

Walking. When walking down the street, heighten your awareness of your whole body. Notice your feet touching the earth. Be aware of your pace and urgency. Scan your body for tension. Let it go. Pay attention to your feelings. Experience the ease and flow of each step. As Tich Nat Han once said, "peace is every step."

Playing with the grandchildren. If you have kids or grandkids, fully embrace their vitality and energy. Get down on their level. Roll on the ground with them. Look deeply into their eyes and notice their innocence. Hug them tightly. Connect with their playfulness and joy.

Meditating. Close your eyes and breathe. Be at one with the universe. Experience the calmness and stillness of the moment. Give thanks for the earth, sun, water, air, and the impossibly improbable opportunity we have to live for a brief period on this earth. Open up your mind. Open up your heart. Expand your spirit. Extend love to those you care about and the larger world. Feel the peace of the moment. Allow yourself to breathe deeply. Welcome whatever comes.

<u>Getting a massage</u>. Experience the warmth and caring of the therapist's hands. Give in to the prodding of each muscle. Enjoy the caressing fingers. Experience the release of tightness. Relax.

<u>Reflecting.</u> Take time to think and explore. Sit quietly and listen. Step out of the rushing rapids and sit calmly on the beach. Let your to-do list take a break. Ponder your possibilities. Look deep inside and ask who you want to be. Listen.

<u>Cheerful greeting.</u> Let people know you are happy to see them. Call out their name. Look into their eyes. Inquire about their lives. Ask genuinely how they are doing. Listen. Respond.

As humans, we have a simple choice in our brief existence on this planet: we can engage in fruitless wars or make love with life. It seems to me that making love offers much fuller possibilities than making war. There are as many ways to make love as there are to fight wars. Let's start expanding the ways we make love and reduce the number of ways we are at war.

Old Friends and New

There's a comfort in old friends. It's a warm, easy comfort that is somehow different from the new. There's no posing, pretending, or pandering. There's no need for anything other than relaxing in the joy of connection and in being who you are. There is no fooling an old friend.

There is a fullness and richness in conversations with old friends. The long histories and specific details of trials, triumphs, and tribulations enrich the re-telling of shared stories and their impact on our lives. I savor those conversations like a steaming, hot cup of chocolate on a cold wintry day. There is a flow and grace that comes from those deep roots. The roots of old friendship are grounded and stabilizing – they have withstood the turbulent storms of our lives. Re-connecting with old friends engenders a relaxed openness that is both soothing and stimulating. Changing contexts and enduring memories are important.

I've been lucky enough to have many friends with whom I have been intimately connected for multiple decades. One of my dearest friends I have known since 1945. We were babies, buddies, and boomers together. We caught frogs, chased snakes, and captured turtles together. We built forts, rope swings, and igloos together. We went to elementary school, high school, and college together. We suffered painful losses together. Spiritually, she has always been at my side and in my heart for my entire life. She is an amazing mom, grandmother, and great-grandmother who has blessed her brood and anyone lucky enough to know her with loving kindness.

Another dear friend I have known since the 50s. We played basketball, ran track, and pursued pretty girls together. He outperformed me in every area. An all-state athlete in three sports, he was also the most popular boy, the strongest leader, and one of the smartest kids in school. He married the high school queen, worked his way through college, and became an extraordinary teacher and coach. We have stayed connected our entire lives. Now, we take great pleasure in beating his son and son-in-law in a yearly golf match. Ahh, the small victories of old age. What I admire most about this friend, however, above and beyond all of his big achievements, is his Zen nature. He lives on 13 acres containing a pond filled with the most delicious blue gills in the world. Every year he brings me a bag of filleted fish, canned fruit, and fresh bounty from his expansive garden. He is equally generous with young kids - overflowing with energy - to old men - in need of a caring hand and heart. We have known each others' kids since they were born. He even let my younger daughter paint his fingernails one day to entertain her. Yes, this man's man wasn't worried enough about his image to keep him from creating a happy experience for a shy kid. In our highly treasured, private conversations, no topic is off limits. His accepting, non-judgmental presence has a calming influence.

I was also lucky enough to meet several people in the 60s with whom I have retained close connections. Three were fraternity brothers in college and two were army buddies from Vietnam – a jarring juxtaposition of two worlds, but still important in different ways. When I get together with the fraternity brothers every couple of years, there are endless tears of laughter from re-counting the silly, superficial, and sophomoric pranks we thrilled in taking. When I get together with my army buddies, there are tears of sadness and dismay from re-counting the stupid, scary, and scandalous errors our country has made and continues to make by starting wars around the world that we can not finish and by causing unimaginable pain and suffering for our own troops and the innocent civilians who are left with the ravages and remains of war. There is great comfort, however, in both sets of connections. I returned with one friend to Vietnam 40 years after we left to say we're sorry for the atrocities we were a part of there and to wonder in the prosperous revival of one of the most gracious and beautiful cultures I have ever witnessed. I have reconnected with another Vietnam buddy and exchange ideas and support on a weekly basis. He was one of the original conceptualizers of PTSD, contributed to the construction of the Vietnam Memorial in Washington DC, and wrote an award winning book on Trauma and Transformation – Healing from the War. After a Ph.D. in Clinical Psychology, 40 years of diligent study and self-exploration, and certifications in various esoteric therapies, he has recently founded Energy's Way, a profound practice for creating more harmonious lives in a more peaceful world.

The 70s produced an abundance of friends ranging from married couples to work colleagues. My wife, Bobbitt, and I are still in regular touch with friends we met in the early years of our marriage over four decades ago. And one of my closest and valued friends has been with me through thick and thin for 45 years. His kids are some of my most treasured friends. He was my coach when I worked in jails, my partner in founding Possibilities, Inc., my mentor on many assignments, my teacher of the Fourth Way and other philosophies, my boss in one of my jobs, and always an unwavering friend through good times and difficult times. Having his perspective always available to me has been an invaluable gift in my life. His short, sometimes terse responses contain more wisdom than volumes of books I've read. Another dear friend I acquired through one of Bobbitt's childhood friends whom she married. They divorced after 20 years or so, but Bobbitt and I remain close friends with her and him and his family and with several subsequent significant others. He is a world-renowned pediatric orthopedic oncologist who has great humility and belly-rolling humor. Even though his censoring mechanism is broken, his heart has always been whole and full of love. He is one of the most supportive, caring, self-effacing people I have ever met. Whenever anyone in the family is suffering emotionally or physically, I can count on regular check-ins and support. These gifts are impossible to measure.

In the 80s, I was introduced to a whole new group of fabulously talented and interesting friends. Bobbitt and I joined a book group in 1984 that is continuing to thrive as I write this post. We started with Orwell's book, 1984, and have discussed over 300 books since that initial meeting. We not only learned how each of these couples think, we also learned how they relate to their families and their worlds. We have become deeply connected to every member of the group. The range of books and conversations has varied widely, and we were introduced to literature we would have never found on our own. I have also been fortunate to form cherished and lasting relationships with work colleagues. We have annual dinners with several couples and meet even more regularly with others. These friendships have added immeasurably to our lives.

Friendships change and evolve over time, but there is a steadfastness of long and deep connections that stabilize our lives, give us hope, and keep us going. I am so grateful for all of these people in my life, beyond family, who enrich me with their loving kindness and caring support. As Stanley Kunitz says, "all relationships are littered and layered. There have been tough times with all of these friends and the level of connection has varied over time. But with these friends, it's easy to wade through the litter because you know the layers keep getting deeper.

New friends open up new worlds as well. I continue to meet people who give me insights and create experiences that I couldn't even have imagined without them. Bobbitt and I have travelled to both poles with one such friend and we have developed a deep and caring connection with her whole family. We meet every summer to see wonderful movies, eat fine food, taste exquisite wine, and simply soak up the extraordinary beauty of Northern Michigan. We have also had the good fortune of having two of the finest, most genuine people you could ever ask for as neighbors at the end of our block in Michigan. He has been patient with my impatience, tolerant of my endless desire to cram one more thing into the day, forgiving of my insane push for speed on my bike, helpful in creating the BS trail in the woods behind our house, and generous in sharing a good share of the fish he catches because I never do. What unbelievable luck to have neighbors like these. There are so many others, unmentioned here, who have graced our lives with their presence. We are daily grateful for the profound impact of their gifts and love in our lives.

As I grow older, I hope to maintain and strengthen my relationships with old friends and new ones. I find hope and faith in my experience of these beautiful connections.

There's a comfort in old friends and an excitement of unforeseen possibilities with new friends. Life is good my friends. I love you all.

Science and Spirituality
Bridges or Barriers to God

Most religions preach that both science and spirituality are barriers to God. Science creates doubts, and spirituality offers an alternative path that doesn't require contributions to the church coffers or preachers' egos. While some spiritual paths may take you off into the weeds or into mountain caves, others offer legitimate ways to tap into higher power, higher purpose, and higher energy.

A recent book by Deepak Chopra and Leonard Mlodinow, *Wars of Worldviews: Where Science and Spirituality Meet – and Do Not,* frames the debate and articulates the argument in substantive and captivating ways, both pro and con, why many people see only the differences between the two points of view. Mlodinow presents the case for science by emphasizing the need for evidence, observation, rigorous analysis, impartial objectivity, quantitative results, statistical proof, and openness to new findings. Chopra presents the case for spirituality by pointing out that life is qualitative as well as quantitative and is subjective as well as objective. He suggests that meaning, spontaneity, free-will, richness of experience, purpose, intention, mindfulness, and consciousness are all elements of spirituality and can't be measured in material ways. It seems to me that science is looking primarily at the "what" of life and spirituality is focused primarily on the "why" of life. The real debate is how the brain, mind, spirit and soul interact – is the mind a manifestation of the brain or can the mind "instruct" the brain what to do. Clearly, there are huge differences among people regarding the extent to which we live our lives unconsciously, numb and asleep or consciously awake and aware.

In my book, *Being at Home in the Universe*, I suggest that all of us have three operating systems (physical, emotional, and intellectual) that get us through life habitually and sub-consciously without us having to make conscious decisions for every choice we confront. The only question is, do we have a CEO (spiritual essence or soul) that is making conscious decisions and giving instructions to the independently operating sub-systems on meaningful choices and mindful intentions.

In the last 20 years there have been major breakthroughs in science about how the brain works and where thoughts, feelings and physical movements get their instructions. A colleague of mine, Due Quach, the founder of Calm Clarity, teaches the scientific basis for our physical, emotional, and intellectual responses in life to inner city, under-privileged kids.

She suggests that by consciously modifying thoughts, emotions and behaviors, we can stimulate specific parts of the brain and, with effort, build neural pathways that support learning and well-being. The key areas to train and develop are the prefrontal cortex which is the center of higher processing, planning, learning, regulation, and willpower, as well as the amygdala and hippocampus.

The amygdala plays a role in processing emotions and encoding memories. The amygdala has a key role in conditioning subconscious responses to sensory stimuli and triggers the flight or fight response to stress. The hippocampus is the primary area of the brain for memory. My point is that we know a great deal about what is going on in the brain, but that doesn't answer the question of how or why, i.e. is the mind controlling the brain or the brain controlling the mind and for what purpose.

As recently as 20 years ago scientists who even wanted to investigate consciousness, would be looked on skeptically by the scientific community. Now whole conferences are devoted to consciousness and are attended by neuroscientists, quantum physicists, philosophers, and yes, spiritual gurus. As a result, we have made tremendous gains in the fields of neuroplasticity and quantum physics as they relate to elevated consciousness.

I believe, however, that scientific imperialism has dominated this discussion and limited the debate to objective, quantifiable studies of the physical dimension of life; and it has erected barriers to investigating the qualitative, subjective possibilities for the emotional and spiritual dimensions of life. Similarly, spirituality flakes have focused primarily on esoteric ideas and have eschewed scientific methodology to test their beliefs, assumptions, and conclusions about life before and after death. I believe there is an opportunity to combine the best of science and spirituality and thus build a newly constructed, and scientifically based, bridge to God - not the tower of Babel but a new pathway to possibilities.

Speaking of God, let's deal with that. Yes, I believe in Universal Energy, Cosmic Connection, Ultimate Mystery, and Infinite Possibility, Intelligence, and Consciousness. To me, those wonders are God. I do not believe in a paternalistic, interventionist, church-created, Puppet Master. I do not know what happens after death. But I do know that I want to strive every day for Near Life Experiences that infuse me with energy, purpose, love, peace, equanimity, gratitude, meaning, and spontaneity so that my consciousness evolves to the highest level possible and I bring more of me to every moment.

Yes, I believe spirituality and science can be bridges to God, not barriers.

Narratives

The power of belief is not necessarily related to the strength of evidence. People create different stories from the same set of facts, but the truth does not necessarily rest in the middle. In most cases, it rests wherever the science is, where the evidence is, where the facts are. That's probably not in the middle. I wish we would quit having debates based on inferences, assumptions, beliefs, and stories and start having them on science-based research whenever and wherever that science exists. And I wish we were more open to debate about spiritual possibilities where the science doesn't exist. Granted, science is always evolving and it can't answer all esoteric questions. That is not an excuse, however, to turn our back on science when it does have an abundance of evidence. Likewise, it is not an excuse to turn our back on spiritual possibilities where the science is still evolving. Ah, the mucky nature of it all.

Let's start with an obvious example. There is an abundance of evidence that tax cuts for the wealthy don't translate to greater revenues for government or income for the poor. As Paul Krugman points out, "the Kansas debacle shows that tax cuts don't have magical powers. The real lesson from Kansas is the enduring power of bad ideas, as long as those ideas serve the interests of the right people."

Krugman continues, "Why, after all, should anyone believe at this late date in supply-side economics, which claims that tax cuts boost the economy so much that they largely, if not entirely, pay for themselves? The doctrine crashed and burned

two decades ago, when just about everyone on the right —
after claiming, speciously, that the economy's performance
under Ronald Reagan validated their doctrine — went
on to predict that Bill Clinton's tax hike on the wealthy
would cause a recession if not an outright depression. What
actually happened was a spectacular economic expansion."

Paul Krugman is seen by folks on the right as an extreme
liberal. If you were to ask conservatives to espouse their
narrative on tax cuts, they would present a very compelling
case – witness their success in influencing current tax policy.
The fact that they can construct a compelling narrative,
however, even one in which they genuinely believe (or not),
doesn't mean their narrative represents the truth. And while
it may not be wise to believe 100% of what Krugman says,
his point of view is clearly (based on evidence from science
and history) much closer to the truth than conservative
economists who are bent on improving their positioning,
power, and personal prosperity.

Joseph Stieglitz, in the Opinionator Section of the New York
Times, expands on this point:

> "If it is not the inexorable laws of economics that have led
> to America's great divide, what is it? The straightforward
> answer: our policies and our politics. People get tired of
> hearing about Scandinavian success stories, but the fact
> of the matter is that Sweden, Finland and Norway have
> all succeeded in having about as much or faster growth
> in per capita incomes than the United States and with
> far greater equality.

So why has America chosen these inequality-enhancing policies? Part of the answer is that as World War II faded into memory, so too did the solidarity it had engendered. As America triumphed in the Cold War, there didn't seem to be a viable competitor to our economic model. Without this international competition, we no longer had to show that our system could deliver for most of our citizens.

Ideology and interests combined nefariously. Some drew the wrong lesson from the collapse of the Soviet system. The pendulum swung from much too much government there to much too little here. Corporate interests argued for getting rid of regulations, even when those regulations had done so much to protect and improve our environment, our safety, our health and the economy itself.

But this ideology was hypocritical. The bankers, among the strongest advocates of laissez-faire economics, were only too willing to accept hundreds of billions of dollars from the government in the bailouts that have been a recurring feature of the global economy since the beginning of the Thatcher-Reagan era of "free" markets and deregulation.

Again, if we were to ask someone from Fox News or the Wall Street Journal about the right size of government, we would get an entirely different point of view. The point is that we construct different narratives out of the same set of facts. Sometimes the narratives are connected to the truth; sometimes they are not.

On a personal level, we do the same thing. Two people can have the same experience and walk away with entirely different stories of what happened. This is due to different personalities, values, experiences, interests, preferences, orientations, or capabilities – physically, emotionally, intellectually, or spiritually. Parents, for example, may view themselves as supportive, fair, genuine, and loving. Children may view those same parents as judgmental, unfair, inauthentic, and uncaring. And both can create narratives that support their beliefs. I'm not sure who gets to determine which side is closer to the truth.

I am struck by the enduring power of bad ideas or convoluted narratives, as long as those ideas and narratives serve private needs or the interests of the rich. I struggle not only with the scientific basis for my own narratives, but also with the sources and science which informs others' narratives. What seems clear to me is that the forcefulness and cleverness with which a narrative is expressed does not equate to its veracity.

States and Stages
Discovery and Development

I just completed an on-line course through MindValley Institute entitled Beyond Seeking taught by Ken Wilber whom I mentioned in a previous post, Spiritual Awakening. The course triggered so many ideas that I wanted to filter them through my lens and write a post. So here it is.

As the title of this post indicates, we can experience many stages and many states. As indicated earlier, I constructed scales for Wilber's four constructs of grow up, show up, wake up, and clean up. Each level on the scales represents a distinct, developmental stage.

The five stages of growing up are: Magical Thinking, Mythological Thinking, Rational Thinking, Inclusive Thinking, and Integral Thinking. This scale enables us to diagnose and develop intellectual functioning – our own and others. Are we assuming things will turn out the way we want because we wish it to be so, or are we actively seeking interdependent relationships and creating integral systems to make things happen?

The five stages of showing up are: It, I, You, We, and THIS. This scale enables us to diagnose and develop our social functioning. Are our individual actions only focused on material accumulation or are we working together to create magical experiences and loving, joyful communities?

The five stages of waking up are: Asleep, Dreaming, Awake, Conscious, and Unified. This scale enables us to diagnose and develop our spiritual functioning. Are we going through life numb and armored or are we embracing and promoting universal connectedness?

The five stages of cleaning up are: Dis-ownership, Repression, Acknowledgement, Dealing (with our own shit), and Using (all experiences that come our way). This scale enables us to diagnose and develop our emotional functioning (or EQ as it is popularly referred to these days.) A parallel emotional scale could be: Non-Attending, Attending, Responding, Personalizing, and Initiating. Whatever scale we use, the question is, "are we defensively rejecting responsibility for all of our actions or are we learning and growing in every moment?

Those scales can give us a sense of where we are and where we need to be regarding our Intellectual, Social, Spiritual, and Emotional Development. Independent of where we are on those stage scales, however, the levels don't automatically inform our State of Being or level of consciousness in any given moment. Meditators or gurus may reach transcendental states of being, but function at very low levels intellectually, socially, or emotionally. That is why many gurus turn out to be corrupt or disappointing. They have spent all their time in a cave and never paid attention to their development. Who can guess what they might have known, if only they had grown.

Essentially, our State of Being is our Essence. As Taoism suggests, an enlightened state or essence is already within us – we just need to open up and find it.

High functioning stages, on the other hand, are developed – we need to make effort to move up the scales. States of Being, therefore, must be seen in the context of the stages. Thus, the two paths to enlightenment are discover and develop. This principle will be valuable the next time you choose a guru.

An old Chinese proverb says: "Chase two rabbits, catch none." Search diligently for masters in states and stages. We not only need maps of development and paths up the scale, we also need the right master to help us rediscover our essence. And our path needs to take into account our level of functioning as well as the teacher's level of functioning.

Each stage of development offers a higher and deeper perspective. Each state of being represents a deeper awareness. I can have a similar state as everyone else, but I am the only one seeing the world from my unique perspective. I am at One and Unique at the same time.

So, that's my summary of life. What about death? Is death a stage or a state? Is "I Am" eternal? Does our witness die? How does cellular connection play in? If I Am at one with the mountain does that mean I'm immortal? Is there any evidence of past lives? Well, the Dalai Lama, for one, doesn't remember past lives, but that doesn't mean it's not possible. The Tibetans may have the most sophisticated spiritual system to address these questions. They maintain that the human being has an essence at the heart that is everlasting through all eternity. While the drop of this lifetime contains all the memories of this lifetime, it dies when our body dies. The drop within, however, contains the sum total of our wisdom (capacity to see emptiness) and the sum total of our virtue (all the good things we did minus all the bad things we did – our ethical, virtuous, or moral resume). When we are born we are carrying with us all our accumulated wisdom and virtue. We just need to discover it. When we die, we lose our memories, but our virtuous resume may appear again in another life. I have no idea what the truth is, but I like this possibility.

Research has shown that kids interacting with adults act differently independent of their environment. Some kids in loving families become mass murderers. Some kids in toxic environment turn out fine. The lion's share of development lies within the infant. Kids who come into this world with a large repertoire of wisdom and virtue have the potential to develop faster. That thought ought to take a little of the pressure off from us parents. We are responsible for nurturing growth, but we can't take full responsibility for how our children turn out. Life and death are mysteries.

Another word for mystery is emptiness. It's a way to free ourselves from the world instead of being sucked into a belief system. Getting in touch with mystery frees us from being locked into or armored down, and it lets us drop any specific belief to which we have been attached. It opens us up to a vast, infinite consciousness without characteristics. It's the fundamental foundation for everything. It's not a system to get us into something, it is a path to get us out of fixed ideas or beliefs. It opens us to new, vast possibilities and keeps us always open to new truths and realities. Learning a development system can help us until it starts to limit us. Hold the system lightly and gently. Don't hold on so tightly you get caught. It's the ultimate escape plan. Rumi asked, "how do I escape this prison for the drunks." Here is a potential answer: make every effort to move up the stages of development, but don't get so caught in the system that you lose track of your State of Being.

Humans have evolved over many millennia, about 200 in fact. Evolution is spirit in action. In the last few hundred years, however, there has been a significant shift. Huxley said, in summarizing Darwin, "evolution became aware of itself." Stages and states are evolution unfolding. We are more aware how we develop, evolve, and grow. It has become part of our awareness. Mythology tries to fix things in place and make them static. The higher stages or development, though, are dynamic - increasingly so as we move up through the stages. Even evolution may turn out to be fixed. We may need to open up to a flowing, dynamic, ever unfolding energy. Paying attention to stages and states may be a good place to start. Develop your highest potential stage. Discover your original state.

Two Dimensional Taoism

What a jarring juxtaposition. My wife and I had just spent 10 days hiking in the natural beauty of Yosemite, Zion, and Bryce National Parks. We ended this delightful vacation with a one-night layover in Las Vegas — the capital of decadent artificiality. It shocked our systems and sensibilities to move so abruptly from the real to the unreal. Ironically, I had also spent the evenings of our day hikes on the spectacularly beautiful trails of our stunning parks editing a 1,000 page translation of the Tao Te Ching by my qigong master of 20 years, Luke Chan. So, for ten straight days and nights, I was totally immersed in the real and natural beauty of nature, in our current times, as well as in the philosophy of the natural flow of life described 2,600 years ago by Laotzu. So the shock was profound when we entered the unreal, glitzy, dazzling insanity of Las Vegas.

Luke had worked for over 10 years on the monumental effort of translating the Tao Te Ching into an accessible and thoroughly researched version of this timeless document. He not only studied the Chuang-tzu translation, but also poured diligently over several other translations including the Ho and Wang translated versions of the text. He organized his book into the Eight Secrets of Tao Te Ching, the English translation of Chuang-tzu quotes, the verbatim translations of Ho Shang Kung and Wang Pi, and a concordance of dictionary definitions of Chinese characters. In the introduction to his book, Luke writes:

"It is time for all us to wake up. Let's be reminded of something we already know: That simplicity has power; self-reliance has power; loving ourselves has power to bring happiness; loving others has the power to bring peace; loving nature has the power to ensure our children and their children have a fair chance to live.

To survive we must change the old way of thinking that has created the problems of today to a new way of thinking for the solution of tomorrow. "See beauty in the ordinary; embrace simplicity." Laotzu's words have been echoing through space and time for thousands of years. The Tao of the old can be a solution for today's excesses and greed."

According to Luke, The purpose of Tao Te Ching is to teach the world to live harmoniously through the Tao of long life. The Tao Te Ching sets out to answer eight important questions:

1. Where do we come from and where are we going?
2. Can the opposite of a profound truth also be true?
3. What is the invisible action wuwei (Can a flap of the wings of a butterfly in one place cause a tornado in another)?
4. What happens when we reach total silence?
5. Are we born enlightened beings?
6. Is there cosmic justice?
7. What is enough?
8. Are we altruistic in nature?

Categorizing the answers to the above questions, Tao Te Ching can be grouped into eight principles or secrets:

1. Tao; 2. Oneness; 3. Action; 4. Silence; 5. Life; 6. Peace; 7. Contentment; 8. Love.

Much has been written about the Tao Te Ching, but no one, before Luke, had made the effort to take into account the most scholarly interpretations of the text. One of the most popular accounts of Taoism is the <u>Tao of Physics</u>, by Fritjof Capra. In this book he suggests that Taoists see all changes in nature as manifestations of the dynamic interplay between polar opposites yin and yang, and thus they came to believe that any pair of opposites constitutes a polar relationship where each of the two poles is dynamically linked to each other. For the Western mind, this idea of the implicit unity of all opposites is extremely difficult to accept. In the East, however, it has always been considered as essential for attaining enlightenment to go beyond earthly opposites.

When I spent a month in China studying qigong with Luke, he would usually spend the afternoons discussing the principles of Taoism. I would take copious notes and type up my impressions in the evening. Here are some of the principles that came clear to me during that intensive time with Luke, and which I included in my book <u>Being at Home in the Universe</u>.

1. Love each other
2. Love interdependence: We are One. Everything is related
3. Greet each day with gratitude
4. Share what you have: Enough is enough. The world is for everyone
5. Love peace
6. Live life fully

7. Silently keep the center
8. Connect with the cosmos
9. Seize the moment
10. Make effort
11. Trust in the universe. Find the gift in the good and the bad
12. Return to the enlightened being of your infancy
13. Anticipate and prepare
14. Stand up for yourself, others, and the environment
15. Laugh at success and failure
16. Grow perspective

In spite of the intuitive "rightness" of these principles, many people are unable to accept or understand the Tao Te Ching because they think it was designed to fool people into accepting the authority of leaders. Some of the most "controversial" principles that stand out in the Tao Te Ching revolve around the call to be simple, soft, and to not accept conventional thinking, rational knowledge, or accumulated wisdom. But, of course, soft is like water and has lots of power if one can use it. And, according to Occam's razor, the most profound solution to a complex problem is sometimes the simplest one. I don't' think the intention of the Tao Te Ching and Taoism is to advocate for one-sided points of view. Indeed, the core of Chinese philosophy is yin (shady side) and yang (sunny side) – that we find each in the other. All of the research and experience I have had points to the need for two dimensions of human behavior: responsive and initiative, nurturing and demanding, conditional and unconditional, supportive and directive, and yes - soft and hard as well as simple and complex. I believe it is important to convey this two dimensional requirement we have as humans to live productively, peacefully, harmoniously, and prosperously.

For me, I had a hard time finding anything but yang in the National Parks and anything but yin in Las Vegas. I guess if I were a true Taoist I would be able to see that there may be some "bad" in the National Park system and some "good" in the Las Vegas culture. Sometimes it's just hard to find either when we have a one-sided point of view.

The Consciousness Solution

Over the course of human history there have been on-going discussions from a variety of sources (religious, social, political, etc.) about how nice it would be if our global civilization could be more compassionate, empathic, loving, harmonious, interdependent and enlightened. Many of these pleas were aimed at reducing lawlessness, preventing wars and saving our souls. While those arguments and reasons for a more compassionate civilization are still compelling and valid, it is no longer just a "nice thing to do." Creating a new platform for civilization is now a requirement for our survival. We need to elevate our dominant processing modes from physical security and tribal compliance to empathic love, harmonious inclusion, and enlightened service. This should have been taught in Sanity 101 decades ago, but it's not too late. Thus the need for the consciousness solution.

What is it? The state of being conscious; an acute awareness of one's own existence, sensations, thoughts, feelings, and intentions. Collectively, consciousness refers to the thoughts and feelings of an aggregate of people, e.g. the moral consciousness of a group, organization, or nation. Consciousness is a loosely defined concept that addresses the human awareness of both internal and external stimuli. This can refer to spiritual recognition, psychological understanding, medically altered states, or more modern-day concepts of life purpose, satisfaction, and self-actualization.

What does it do? Heightened consciousness increases the full activity of the mind and senses; it awakens the body, mind and spirit; it makes one more aware of awareness. It enables us to bring more of all of ourselves to each moment.

Why is it important? Consciousness increases internal and external knowledge and the sense of what's right and wrong; it elevates perspective, quickens development and sharpens the sense of justice; it broadens and deepens the view of our lives and our role in the universe; it contributes to peaceful co-existence.

How does it work? Most theories map consciousness into a series of levels, some stages of which are more continuous or complex than others. Movement between stages is often bidirectional depending on internal and external conditions, with each mental ascension precipitating a change in reactivity. In the most basic sense, this alteration might lead to a reduced responsiveness as seen in anesthesiology; more abstract facets of tiered consciousness describe characteristics of insight, perception, or understanding. There are multiple ways to increase levels of consciousness, the most common of which are meditation, yoga, qigong, energy's way, and the science of possibilities.

Based on an extensive review of the research in consciousness, I developed the following scale:

7: **Enlightened Service** (transcendent and universal, wholistic reality, spontaneous expression, at one, super awake and aware of being aware)
6: **Harmonious Inclusion** (unified, at peace, interdependent, awake and aware)
5: **Empathic love** (psychological affiliation, in touch, in tune, collaborative)

4: **Logical thinking** (ideological and achievement oriented, calculated, independent)

3: **Tribal compliance** (religious, political, or social conformity, competitive)

2: **Physical security** (naïve and mythological, imposed, controlling)

1: **Survival instinct** (reactive and ego-centric, unconscious, dependent, asleep, unaware)

At level one, Survival Instinct, we are essentially reactive, ego-centric, asleep, unconscious, and dependent on others. If you see the world through the lens of level 1 consciousness, then everyone looks like the enemy. The implications of seeing and being in the world at this level of consciousness are that there is more likelihood to get embroiled in wars, to focus on profits and ideology instead of making sure everyone has a right to decent health care, to deny education based on gender, race, and class, to engage in abusive labor practices whether it's slavery or toxic working conditions, and to refuse to take responsibility for protecting mother earth. Trying to convince someone with selfish interests and a survival mentality that their behaviors are limiting and ultimately self defeating is like trying to persuade cave dwellers to enjoy a little sunshine. Saudi Arabia and North Korea are examples of nations whose collective consciousness could be characterized as level one.

At level two, Physical Security, we are essentially acquisitive, controlling, and possessive. We engage in mindless accumulation. The world is viewed in terms of safety and control. If you see the world through the lens of level 2 consciousness, then everything looks like an opportunity or threat to your personal needs. At this level, we are more likely to impose our beliefs, values, and points of view on others and may even have a mythological view of the world, i.e. imaginary or assigning truth to fiction. The implication of seeing and being in the world at this level of consciousness is that there is essentially a state of denial. People at this level ignore or deny overwhelming evidence of scientific discoveries, inequalities, global warming trends, and inadequate health care for the majority of the population. Also, the primary goal of life is acquisition of endless material comforts that reinforce the illusion of safety and control. Pakistan and Afghanistan are examples of nations whose collective consciousness could be characterized as level two.

At level three, Tribal Compliance, we are essentially competitive. The world is viewed through rigid political or religious dogma. Conformity to rules, regulations, rituals, norms, values, and beliefs is the driving force for how people think, relate, and plan. At this level, there is a competitive spirit that motivates people to demonstrate superiority or exclusivity. If you see the world through the lens of level 3 consciousness, then everything looks like evidence to support your beliefs independent of truth or rigorous research. The implications of being in the world at this level of consciousness are constant conflict, special interests compete for resources, exploitation is justified as the price for winning, and there is a cavalier willingness to satisfy individual or group needs at the expense of the environment. These implications lead to a feeling of exceptionalism or the belief that special rules apply because of unique moral authority or righteous values. The United States and China are examples of nations whose collective consciousness could be characterized as level three. Clearly, in the year 2014, the

"United" States is totally divided into political and religious camps whose primary purpose is to undermine and defeat the other side. China belongs here as well for different reasons. China insists on conformity to rules and they are motivated to demonstrate their superiority. They are also guilty of serious human rights violations and exploitative behavior.

At level four, Logical Thinking, we are intellectually oriented. The world is organized through rational, factual, logical, analytic methodology. Even though there is a strong achievement orientation, most decisions are calculated for independent gain or positioning. If you see the world through the lens of level 4 consciousness, then everyone looks like a problem to be solved with estimations of probability based on external, objective data. The implications for seeing and being in the world at this level of consciousness are that there is an openness to constructive intellectual debate, there is a commitment to providing high quality health care with reasonable choice, education emphasizes discriminative learning or increasing the repertoire of responses to any stimulus, the economy is driven by a compassionate capitalism, and there are national agreements on measures that need to be taken to protect the environment. Many countries in the European Union can be characterized as level four.

At level 5, Empathic Love, we are essentially collaborative. The world is experienced as possibilities for affiliation and connection. There is a genuine desire to be in touch with and in tune with others. If you see the world through the lens of level 5 consciousness, then relationships are viewed as dilemmas to be managed in nuanced and layered ways.

The implications for seeing and being in the world at this level of consciousness are that dialogue tends to be open, honest, and direct with both thoughts and feelings taken into account. Health care tends to be accessible and affordable, information is processed in human centric ways, prosperity is ubiquitous, and the environment is protected by international agreements. Many of the Scandanavian countries could be characterized as level five.

At level 6, Harmonious Inclusion, the world is experienced as a complex inter-play of interdependent possibilities. People are unified, at peace, awake, and aware. If you see the world through the lens of level 6 consciousness, then everyone is nested in their unique organizational and cultural context. History and context and taken into account in each person's life. The implications for seeing and being in the world at this level of consciousness are that there would be world peace, universal health care, a preventive health orientation, organizational processing, ubiquitous prosperity, and a healthy environment. There would be very little inequality and pollution. Unfortunately, there are few individuals and no current examples of countries with this level of consciousness. Clearly the world is suffering from poverty, pollution, preventable disease, inequality and ignorance. Historically, the approach to these problems has been to chase the symptoms without changing our level of consciousness. As a result, we are spiraling ever more deeply into a sinkhole. The only way out is to change the lens through which we perceive the world so that our elevated perspective enables us to diagnose problems and generate solutions that actually work.

At level 7, Enlightened Service, we are essentially cosmic. The world is viewed through a lens of transcendent possibilities. People see reality wholistically and engage in spontaneous expression. The world is populated with super-awake, super aware people who are at one with the universe. Since the universe is their Home, people live in peace, practice high level wellness, engage in cultural processing, and continuously generate new ideas that provide increased opportunities and prosperity for everyone. Needless to say, the air, water, and sources of energy are all clean and our lakes, streams, and ocean are pristine and vital. We are a long way from that idealized vision of what's possible, but a change in consciousness can help us to move in that direction.

Elevating consciousness requires a change in focus. We need to focus more on the universe, in which the earth represents an infinitesimal dot, and less on our planet as the center of the universe. This shift demands a change in perspective.

We need to focus more on the power of energy and less on the force of matter which represents less than 1% of all space. This shift demands a change in awareness.

We need to focus more on our nothingness and less on the "things" that drive our life. This shift demands a change in orientation.

We need to focus more on our future potential and less on current and past reality. This shift demands a change in thinking from cause and effect to "causing an effect" by raising our level of consciousness. The energy of infinite possibilities is shaped by consciousness. In short, we are a consciousness that is using body and brain for better or for worse. We need to be grateful for possibilities that all these shifts create and be dedicated to making them happen.

In my book, *The Consciousness Solution*, I started with a brief history and overview of consciousness. I then discussed the applications and implications of an elevated consciousness as well as the physical, emotional, intellectual, and spiritual strategies for achieving higher states of being and levels of consciousness. I shared my personal experiences in consciousness raising and provided an example of how technology could accelerate the process. I concluded with a glimpse of the contributions one person has made to elevating consciousness by creating a new platform for civilization built upon the science of possibilities and systems for new capital development.

In the book, I tried to take the reader on a journey from abstract notions of consciousness created in the past to concrete possibilities generated for the future if, and only if, we can raise our level of consciousness.

In conclusion, I believe that if science and technology continue to reinforce levels of consciousness mired in survival instincts, individual security, and tribal instincts, the future of the planet is dim. If, on the other hand, science and technology provide bridges to higher levels of consciousness, then the future is bright. May we choose the latter.

The Centrality Delusion

In 1632, Galileo angered the Pope when he published a book in which he openly stated that the Earth was moving around the Sun. He was put on trial by the Inquisition in Rome, where he was found suspect of heresy, and forced to say that all of his findings were wrong. He was first imprisoned, and later confined to his house near Florence. This event was an early indication that debunking myths around centrality could lead to rather unpleasant consequences. Yes, we like to think we are the center of the universe.

The trend has continued as new myths are being challenged. Yet we humans prefer to believe that we are the reason the universe exists. Unfortunately, evidence to the contrary would suggest otherwise.

Even though we have existed on the earth a small fraction of the earth's life span, we cling to the delusion that we are special. The first animals appeared on the earth over 500 million years ago. Mammals started to evolve almost 200 million years ago. Our human ancestors didn't make their first entrance until around 200,000 years ago.

Yes, this delusion of centrality has a long history. First we thought the earth was the center of the universe, and we still cling to the delusion that humans are special creatures on earth in spite of the fact that we have only lived on this rock in the universe about 1/20,000 of its history.

The story gets worse and more dangerous. As an extension of this notion of centrality, people have become so attached to their tribes, states, and nations that they kill each other to establish superiority and to reinforce their belief that they are somehow special. Wars are fought to extend boundaries and claim rights. Even within states, people identify with particular groups to bolster this delusion. This over-identification gets dangerous when groups are unable to collaborate for the greater good.

The centrality delusion extends to how we view ourselves in our particular groups. There seems to be an over-riding need to stand out, to be the center of attention, to be special. We would prefer to talk about ourselves than to inquire about others. There is a noticeable absence of demonstrating interest in and understanding of others' lives and points of view. As a student of interpersonal relationships for over 40 years, I have plenty of "laboratory" time to support this observation.

All of this discussion is simply context to the major point. We hold onto the delusion that "I am here now and central to my own life." This belief is delusional and dangerous because it leads to the mistaken conclusion that we have a crystallized essence and a magnetic center that is calling the shots in our lives. Recent breakthroughs in neuro-science suggest that we consist of multiple zombie agents that control most of our decisions. These zombie agents or habitual operating systems determine our physical, emotional, and intellectual actions, interactions, and reactions. In short, the notion that our mind controls our brain and that we are exercising free will has been largely debunked by recent scientific discoveries. The Pope may have to raise his ugly head again. After all, no one likes to go from feeling central and in control to feeling like a rather insignificant puppet under the control of zombie agents.

Hopefully, there is a positive side to this rather bleak story. And, we will not have to rely on the Pope to come to the rescue. We need to accept the fact that we are a recent entry on the evolutionary time-line, and that we are largely determined by the survival instincts and habits that we needed to acquire to stay alive as long as we have. Once we accept that fact, we can make great effort to observe our three-brained operating systems and try to establish our own CEO who exercises some choice around how we manifest ourselves in this world. As our CEO emerges and develops, we can exercise the discipline required to connect to our higher selves and to universal energy. This means being obedient to well-defined values and to our purpose: to tap into universal energy and to bring positive influences in the world; to become one with the Universe and to seek commonality instead of centrality; to realize that we are all entwined together in a social fabric that envelops the earth; to accept the limitations of others, but not let those limitations limit us; to forgive the transgressions of centrality in others and in ourselves; to love others and to love ourselves; to do no harm to the earth.

To do otherwise is to continue on the path of destruction that we are currently paving with ever more sophisticated tools and technology. We need to move from delusion to discipline, from centrality to commonality, from callousness to compassion. And we need to be open to the possibility that there is an Infinite Intelligence of which we are a part that gives our lives meaning, purpose, peace, and joy.

The Questions We Live In . . . . or Not

It seems like we are always desperately seeking answers in our life. "If only I could be certain about this," or "I sure wish I knew the answer to that." Unfortunately, when the total quantity of information in the world is **doubling twice a day**, it's going to be increasingly impossible to keep up with all the "answers" that are literally available at our fingertips. It doesn't necessarily mean the answers are getting better, they are just proliferating at an ever increasing rate.

To get a little perspective on how fast information is increasing, until 1900 human knowledge doubled approximately every century. By the end of World War II, knowledge was doubling every 25 years. While the quantity of information is exploding exponentially, the quality of information may not be on the same curve. Here is a scale to evaluate the level of "answers" that are relentlessly bombarding us everyday:

5: Wisdom
4: Creativity
3: Knowledge
2: Information
1: Data

Data are simply random facts. Information is contextualized data, i.e. the data are represented in way that gives some meaning, e.g. elevating facts to concepts. Knowledge is contextualized information. At this level, the information is represented in a way that helps us derive principles – it may show the interrelationship of components, functions, and processes and provide standards and conditions. Creativity is the ability to generate new responses facilitated by the representation of the knowledge. Wisdom is the ability to discern real meaning and value from the creative responses.

While the news media report that knowledge is doubling twice a day, I think it would be more accurate to say that data are doubling twice a day. As you go up the scale, the rate of increase decreases. I don't know how fast information (contextualized data) is increasing. I don't know how fast knowledge (contextualized and well-represented information) is increasing – clearly not as fast as data. I don't know how much better we are at creativity than we were 100 years ago. Clearly, we are confronting different problems, but I don't know if this generation is 10 times more creative than my grandparent's generation. Most importantly, I don't believe we are demonstrating any more wisdom than people in the past. In fact, there is plenty of evidence to indicate that the wisdom curve is on a downward path given the level of pollution, poverty, and violence in the world.

But this post is not about answers, it's about questions. The problems of the world are not caused by a lack of answers, they are caused because we are not living in the right questions.

Since I introduced the 5 point scale, let me use it to categorize the type of questions we might ask at each level:

- **Data Question**: How many gigabytes of data can be stored on this microchip?
- **Information Question**: How much more money can I make in financial services vs. education?
- **Knowledge Question**: How can I become more multi-dimensional, increase the quality of my life, improve my learning agility, and broaden by career skills?
- **Creativity Question**: What if everyone could post pictures of themselves in a public place where the world could access them instantaneously? How might I make all the world's information accessible to everyone on the planet? I wish we could create an even playing field for everyone.
- **Wisdom Question**: How can I bring more of myself to every moment at a higher level of consciousness?

The questions we need to ask ourselves are:

1. At what level on the scale do I find myself asking the most questions?
2. How much of my life do I spend living in the questions at that level?
3. What questions am I asking at that level?
4. Are the answers to these questions giving me a greater sense of meaning in my life?
5. What questions might I consider living in that would lead to a greater sense of meaning?

I believe that living in questions at levels 3, 4, and 5 on the scale are far more likely to lead to a richer, meaningful, and fulfilling life.

The Physics of Consciousness

Since I turned 70, I decided to post a bold article on the possibilities and potential of expanded consciousness. I know I will not be able to maintain my current level of physical health for the next decade, but I'm hoping to grow spiritually in whatever time remains for me.

As one step on that quest, I recently read an article on the *Physics of Consciousness* (Beichler, 2013) which explores how the brain and consciousness relate to one another. Carl Jung once said, "In history, everything depends on consciousness." There are, however, many conflicting views on consciousness, how it can be defined, and its relationship to the brain.

Here are some statements from Beichler's article that triggered a deeper exploration of consciousness for me:

	True	False
External information affects consciousness, which affects mind, which, in turn, affects brain.		
Fields are physical without being material.		
Life force goes beyond ordinary physiology.		
Mind consists of electrical field patterns.		

Consciousness consists of multi-level magnetic vector field patterns.		
Microtobules are magnetic induction coils for storage and retrieval of memories and recognition.		
Consciousness is not limited to the brain.		

I believe all of those statements are true, but to be honest, I wouldn't know a microtubule from a gazoobatuba. (Don't google it; I made it up). I particularly like the idea of higher sources and forces informing our consciousness which, in turn, affect our minds and brains. I believe those forces and sources exist, and I'm beginning to learn through Energy's Way (www.energysway.com) how to tap them.

In his article, Beichler discusses the implications of seeing "self" as 4 or 5 dimensional vs. 3 dimensional. Upon further inquiry from multiple sources, I found that, in mathematics, four-dimensional space ("4D") is a geometric space with four dimensions. It is typically meant to mean four-dimensional Euclidean space, generalizing the rules of three-dimensional models. It has been studied by mathematicians and philosophers for over two centuries, both for its own interest and for the insights it offered into mathematics and related fields.

Algebraically, it is generated by applying the rules of vectors and coordinate geometry to a space with four dimensions. In particular a <u>vector</u> with four elements. The space is a Euclidean space, so it has a metric and norm, and all directions are treated as the same: the additional dimension is indistinguishable from the other three.

In modern physics, space and time are unified in a four-dimensional Minkowski continuum called spacetime, whose metric treats the time dimension differently from the three spatial dimensions.

Clearly, if mathematics and physics can't present a precise view, how can we approach 4D and 5D space from a spiritual point of view? There is agreement that these dimensions exist, we are just not sure what to do with them. For me, the point is that, as 3D beings, we can't see how the world might operate at 4D or 5D. It would be the same as asking a 2D being to view the world in 3D; it can't happen.

To get different perspectives on these issues, I sent Beichler's article to a few friends of mine to get their reactions. Here are excerpts from 3 responses - (all of whom, coincidentally, are Harvard grads):

<u>Friend 1</u>

"There is something like a divine satellite broadcasting across time and space. Human beings definitely have the capacity to receive the broadcast. However, when the message enters a person's field, what's in the field interacts with the broadcast to digest it and translate it into language. What is perceived will be unique to each person. What seems to be happening is that a person puts their own "signature" on the message, such that it can be greatly distorted to affirm a person's existing belief system.

Mystical experiences present enormous challenges for a 3 dimensional brain to behold, take in and describe to another 3 dimensional brain that is wired to process information differently. As I look at the scriptures across religions, I hypothesize that the "revelations" of prophets are exposed to two types of human error: they can be misinterpreted by the prophet and distorted by the language used to retell it. Truth cannot be absolute when retold by brains.

As you may guess, I've been pondering to what degree one can tune-up one's receiving abilities. Can one reduce the distortion created by one's mind translating the broadcast into meaning and words? My guess is that when a person is not attached to any belief system, that person's field may have the ability to perceive without imposing onto what is being seen and most likely what that person sees would transcend doctrine and dogma. The irony is that its rare for atheists to have mystical experiences because they are often not open to them."

Friend 2:

"We can only understand any phenomena at the level we are at; the deeper truths are there all the time if our being and knowledge evolve. Magnetic fields and chi fields are in us and around us. These energy fields hold this world and the universal world. The challenge is to see them and tap them."

Friend 3:

"Beichler unselfconsciously is proceeding as if a mechanics of consciousness is desirable and even possible. For me this issue was settled centuries ago on the grounds that wholes are not explained by parts or substrates. Those who believe otherwise, and that it is worthwhile to try all the same, as in explaining a higher order or emergent phenomenon (consciousness) in terms of its physical components, fields or substrates, are entitled to their path. But their notes to themselves are not interesting to me."

You and I, on the other hand, might have a "meaningful conversation" re: how it might be good and possible to proceed on this topic--beginning with how to translate this "thing" thought of "consciousness" in the light of "energy is action" and the subtlest of all energetic doings, conscious-making, even more so."

In essence, Friend 3 was saying that Beichler made a category mistake in trying to objectify a subjective experience. The term "category-mistake" was introduced by Gilbert Ryle in his book *The Concept of Mind* (1949) to remove what he argued to be a confusion over the nature of mind born from Cartesian metaphysics. Ryle alleged that it was a mistake to treat the mind as an object made of an immaterial substance because predications of substance are not meaningful for a collection of dispositions and capacities.

I found all three of these reactions more compelling and thought provoking than the article itself. Friend 1 made me think about how we can fine-tune our receivers to be able to hear divine broadcasts more clearly. Friend 2 made me consider ways to tap into the magnetic and chi fields that are in us and around us. Friend 3 made me wonder how we can move from an explanation of consciousness to an experience of consciousness (energy is action).

I know that the line between genius and madness is notoriously thin. I am committed to continue looking for the genius without crossing the line into madness. This notion of consciousness brings out our truest possibilities and purposes as well as speculative nonsense with no scientific grounding.

I believe the possibility exists that we have astral bodies that contain both concrete and abstract levels of consciousness. I believe that consciousness is the root and essence of the soul. I also believe we have an etheric body that contains the chakra energy centers and an aura that can expand into the universe. Within the etheric body, the chakras can be activated and aligned. The astral bodies and etheric bodies contain our physical body and inform its development.

I realize I am walking that thin line here, but I have enough experience and I've read enough explanations to feel like I'm simply exploring possibilities instead of entertaining delusions. A recent book by Dean Radin, *Supernormal*, is an excellent review of what our possibilities may be and how conventional thinking has limited our ability to pursue them or even to open the conversation about them. May the conversation and breakthroughs continue.

THIS and that

After reading a plethora of books on science and spirituality, it strikes me that science attempts to explain **things** to us and spirituality encourages us to experience **events** within us. The real conflict between the two is the difference between explanation and experience. Scientists want to explain our experience and spiritualists want us to experience our explanations.

Science is primarily concerned with objective, external, materialistic things. For example, theoretical physicists have done an amazing job of explaining quarks, gluons, bosons etc. in quantum mechanics as well as the relationship of mass and speed of light to energy in Einstein's theory of relativity (E=mc2). In the *Grand Design*, Stephen Hawking provides new insights on time and space with astounding insights into dark matter, dark energy, and how the universe in expanding. Similarly, neuroscientists have achieved incredible breakthroughs on explaining how different components of the brain affect memory, thoughts, feelings, and physical reactions. Indeed, breakthroughs in science have led to new discoveries not only on the origin of the universe, but also on our understanding of our day-to-day behaviors. All of these advances in science give us a deeper and clearer explanation of ancient history and current reality.

The strong bias of science for rationalistic, reductionist approaches to exploration and understanding has contributed significantly to many breakthroughs. I'm grateful for the clarifying explanations of the Big Bang, the discovery of microbes morphing into cells which morphed over a few billion years into all the species and plants on earth, the advances in our understanding of an expanding universe starting with the fact that the earth revolves around the sun, and for all the brain research that helps us understand the functions of the cerebral cortex, the hippocampus, the amygdala, and neurotransmitters. But all of these welcome explanations can not explain human experience. As Kurt Goldstein says, "This vain attempt to explain is made again and again - overlooking the fact that it is quite possible to understand the part on the basis of the whole, but that it is not possible to comprehend the whole on the basis of the parts."

On a personal note, the biggest reasons I went to China for a month to study qigong was to find a path from my head to my heart, to develop the spiritual part of my life, and to experience a greater wholeness.

Spirituality is concerned with subjective, internal, wholistic, immaterial experiences. Just as there have been breakthroughs in science in recent years, there have also been transformative advances in spirituality. Herbert Benson and Joan Borysenko published studies on the mind-body connection in the 80s. John Kabat Zinn and Ellen Langer wrote about the benefits of mindfulness in the 90s. Yoga, transcendental meditation, qigong and Tai Chi became popularized as we entered the new millennium. And now, as we experience events in the second decade of the 21st century, many more breakthroughs are occurring in science and spirituality. One of the most powerful is Energy's Way, developed over 40 years by a Harvard trained psychologist,

Artie Egendorf. Simplistically, he asks us to focus on THIS instead of that.

Essentially, he suggests that we see spirituality as experiencing THIS and view science as explaining that. Why the caps on THIS? Because THIS is the essence of spirituality. Dr. Egendorf writes:

> "saying "this" at once calls you to attend to just what's emerging, here now. And at the same instant draws out and names what "this" calls you to notice. Word, impact, meaning all are intertwined, turning on their own turnings, in a single utterance. And so, whatever else is also true, THIS is Energy's Way. Now, all good work does its work like "this" does: whatever way you find to open, create, evolve, are ways that open to openness, create creating, evolve evolving. And when you're tuned into direct experience what pours in with such turnings-back-on-themselves is energy."

When I read the introduction to Artie's new book, The Genius School, I wrote this poem to capture my meager understanding:

Stop shrinking, numbing, armoring
and start approaching a joyous jazz -
Experience energy's way.
No need for explanation or identification
No need for maps or things -
Just give yourself to spontaneous expression
And grow your aura with each new day.

THIS leads to joyful dance with life; "that" leads to more explanations of how we might think about living our life while we miss living it. Energy's Way encourages us to experience more of THIS and less of "that." It shows us the steps – yes, the science – to dance to the joyous jazz of life.

I have experienced this dance in a very profound way as a result of practicing the 12 steps of Energy's Way for the last 2 years. My life in New York causes me to walk 5-10 miles per day. My habituated way of walking was to set a wicked pace and be unaware of any part of my body other that my feet going as fast as they could. I would carry a great deal of tension in my shoulders, neck, and face. As I began to become more conscious of each step and to experience my feet touching the ground, the tension began to melt away, and I experienced a new lightness that I had never noticed or experienced before. One would think I would have learned to walk in the first 7 decades of my life. I hadn't.

If you want to check this out, watch how freely and loosely a baby crawls and walks. There is a natural turning and tuning with each move – an openness to each new experience. Then watch someone who has gone through the mill of life and notice the difference. Probably you will see tightness, tension – maybe even a shrinking and armoring. Most importantly, observe yourself as you walk. Notice the tightness. Notice the tension. Lighten up. Experience THIS, forget about that.

Transcendent Possibilities

My hunch is that we are all searching for transcendental possibilities, but what in hell does that mean? I have been on a long journey trying to figure out what those possibilities might look like and how I can have any real degree of assurance that what people claim can be true. Thirty-two years ago I co-founded Possibilities, Inc. with Barry Cohen, a PhD philosopher, as a discovery vehicle for this journey. I've covered a lot of ground since that time, but instead of finding a crystal clear, scientifically sound, and personally pristine answer, I keep finding more gray theory. It seems I am not alone in this search. In the last few months, I have read several books making claims and articulating positions In this space. Here are a few of the most provocative and enlightening:

Waking Up, by Sam Harris
Mind and Cosmos, by Thomas Nagel
Phi, A Voyage from the Brain to the Soul, by Giulio Tononi
The Tao of Physics, by Fritzof Capra
The Particle at the End of the Universe, by Sean Carroll
A Religion of One's Own, by Thomas Moore
Qigong meets Quantum Mechanics, by Imke Boch-Mobius

As you can see by the titles and the authors, this space has attracted neuroscientists, theoretical physicists, philosophers, psychologists, and spiritualists. As more and more people reject religion as irrelevant, there is an increasing demand for transcendence without dogmatic baggage.

Richard Bellingham

In this post, I will summarize what I found to be the most intriguing points from each of the books above and then throw my own opinion into the mix.

<u>Waking up</u>: In this book, Sam Harris implores us to talk about spirituality in rational terms – acknowledging the validity of self-transcendence – and suggests that transcendent spirituality is essential for this world if it is going to avoid being shattered by dogmatism. Harris shares his experiences with psychedelic drugs and narcissistic gurus in the East and West. In this surprising follow-up book to his best selling *End of Faith*, he continues his blistering attack on religion and summarizes his beliefs as follows: "Religion is a set of stories that recount the ethical and contemplative insights of our wisest ancestors. But these stories come to us bundled with ancient confusion and perennial lies. And they harden into doctrines that defy revision, generation after generation." In this book, Harris suggests that meditation and mindfulness are more likely to flourish on a non-religious path and yield more peaceful and productive results. Harris argues that consciousness is simply the light by which the contours of mind and body are known. It is that which is aware of thoughts and feelings but can never be improved or harmed by what it knows. Making this discovery, again and again, is the basis of spiritual life.

<u>Mind and Cosmos</u>: In this book, Thomas Nagel claims the widely held view of most scientists and philosophers, who comment on the natural order, is that reductive materialism is the only serious possibility. Nagel rejects that argument and finds it highly implausible that life as we know it is the result of a sequence of physical accidents together with the mechanism of natural selection. On the road to higher levels

of consciousness, Nagel implores us to consider an alternative between dogmatic religiosity and scientific reductionism.

Phi: In this book, Giulio Tononi discusses the role of each part of the brain in consciousness. He defines consciousness as integrated information (phi) that comes from all areas of the brain. In the conclusion, Tononi suggests that the more we know and understand, the more phi grows and breathes. He goes on to posit that consciousness is maximally irreducible and unique. He suggests that consciousness is the shape of understanding, the only shape that's really real – the most real thing there is. Consciousness is a model of how the world might be, a model built over millions of years, with immense sacrifice at the expense of innumerable losses, paid for by endless wars, won by the sweat of slaves, mended by lessons, polished by civilizations, schools, and learned arguments. But it's a model woven in the only language we own, that of the brain and its enchanted loom. Without the inner glow of consciousness, there would be no sight. What we must do is go and seek the light, the light that unifies. In his summary, Tononi challenges us to grow, share, and connect in order to heighten our consciousness.

The Tao of Physics: In this classic book, originally published in 1975, Fritzof Capra discusses the parallels of subatomic physics with eastern mysticism and shares the realization that the constituents of matter and the basic phenomena involving them are all interconnected, that they cannot be understood as isolated entities but only as integral parts of a unified whole. The notion of a basic quantum interconnectedness reinforces the similarities between the views of physicists and mystics and raises the intriguing possibility of relating subatomic physics to psychology. In addition to showing how non-local entanglement relates to humans as well as atoms, Capra also provides a remarkably clear and concise summary of Hinduism, Buddhism, Taoism, and Zen.

<u>The Particle at the End of the Universe</u>: In this book, Sean Carroll summarizes the most recent findings in particle physics. He reviews the systematic, worldwide effort to discover the basic rules governing how the universe works. Particle physics arises directly from our restless desire to understand our world; it's not the particles that are particularly motivating, but the human desire to figure out what we don't understand. Carroll reveals the amazing commitment of scientists around the world to discover the Higgs boson – how they did it and why they did it. He provides a comprehensive and comprehensible explanation of non-local entanglement and wave theory. These discoveries help us understand that we are more energy than matter. It's up to us to figure out how to mobilize that energy.

<u>A Religion of One's Own</u>: In this book, Thomas Moore, (the author of *Care of the Soul, Soul Mates,* and *The Soul's Religion*) provides a guide for creating personal spirituality in a secular world. In the face of rapidly changing and, in many areas, disappearing religion, Moore proposes a religion essentially and radically reimagined for our time. He defines religion as our creative and concrete response to the mysteries that permeate our lives. His intent is to deepen our understanding of the religious traditions while acknowledging that formal religions can get in the way of the deep religion he is seeking. Moore goes on to define soul as the unreachable depth, the felt vitality, and full presence of a person or even a thing. It is the invisible, mysterious, and softly radiant element that infuses your being and

makes you human. Like plasma in your veins, it gives you a sense of meaning, feeling, connection, and depth.

<u>Qigong meets Quantum Physics</u>: This book succeeds in presenting both an easily accessible outline of quantum physics and also an appreciation of mysticism beyond vagueness and obscurity. From here it describes the physical and mental movements of qigong as a way of integrating body and mind, head and heart, detailing specific exercises and outlining their rationale and effects.

So, what do I take from all of this. While most neuroscientists (e.g. Eagleman, Koch, etc.) believe that when the brain dies consciousness dies with it and there is no soul that goes to a different place, I still hold onto my beliefs that we can develop a soul on earth, we can reach transcendental states of Oneness, and there is a Nameless Source and Force that operates in the world. I also appreciated Tononi's message in *Phi, A Voyage from the Brain to the Soul,* in which he cleverly demonstrates how different parts of the brain function and how integrated information (Phi) can emerge from all components of the brain, e.g. cerebellum, cerebral cortex, hippocampus, and amygdala.

While most theoretical physicists are in the scientific, materialistic reduction camp, there are some intriguing possibilities that are emerging from that research. Specifically, the idea of non-local entanglement demonstrates that once two cells come in contact with each other, they remain interconnected independent of location or time. Also, continuing breakthroughs in particle physics are shedding light on the role of waves and the relationship between energy and matter. It seems to me that entanglement and energy play extremely important roles in spiritual development. We are more inter-connected than we thought and energy is more important than matter.

For me, it all boils down to consciousness. I like two definitions of consciousness that came from the books reviewed above. In *Phi*, Tononi defines consciousness as the shape of understanding, the only shape that's really real – the most real thing there is. In *Waking Up*, Harris defines consciousness as the light by which the contours of mind and body are known. It is that which is aware of thoughts and feelings but can never be improved or harmed by what it knows. I also like Gurfjieff's idea (not summarized above) of crystallized essence which simply (or not simply) means that we can become more unified and conscious over time if we make efforts to observe ourselves and pay close attention to the thoughts, feelings, and instincts that pop up in our bodies and minds in every situation. One of my favorite lines from Gurdjieff is, "never say I and think it is you."

Harris bangs on this point as well in *Waking Up*. He claims there is no I and no self. When we get beyond that (i.e. no ego, no "self behind the eyes), we have a chance for self- transcendence. Gurdjieff also pushes us to let go of imagination (thinking we are more than what we are, identification (thinking of ourselves as a Dr., lawyer, teacher, etc.,) hiding behind the role and negative emotion (forgetting that every moment is the most improbable gift you could imagine). To me, these are additional ways of clinging to the idea of a "self." We need to open up, lighten up and let go.

Even though I believe "THIS" all boils down to consciousness, I don't believe consciousness is an easy state to attain. Gurdjieff suggests there are seven levels of development with consciousness being the next to last rung on the scale:

7.0: Perfected
6.0: Conscious
5.0: Unified
4.0: Balanced
3.0: Intellectual
2.0: Emotional
1.0: Physical

Very few of us are balanced, much less unified. Most of us are physically, emotionally, or intellectually oriented with relative deficits in one of two of the other areas. Hopefully, after much work, we can become more balanced and unified, i.e. our hearts, minds, and bodies are singing in harmony. Being conscious occurs rarely – probably when effort becomes effortless. In history, perhaps a few of our great ancestors achieved perfection by the end of their lives. My goal is to experience a few moments of being unified and conscious in my lifetime.

Given all that, here's where I come out. I accept the research from theoretical physicists and neuroscientists who are finding that we are interconnected and filled with energy. I accept the fact that when our bodies and brains die, we will no longer have the memories or identities that we carry around on earth. Finally, I still believe that we can develop a soul (crystallized essence, integrated information) and that we can achieve higher levels of consciousness. When making effort becomes effortless, we may also realize transcendent possibilities.

Being at Home in the Universe

An Internal Space or an External Refuge

At my older daughter's wedding, she sang the song, "Feels Like Home to Me" to her husband. It struck me that we are all searching for a sense of home in our lives, and I was so grateful that she had found a man with whom she felt at home. Her beautiful voice filled the reception hall and my hope for everyone there was that they felt, in that moment, that they were home.

After several years of reflection on what HOME really means, I came to the conclusion that we search for HOME in all the wrong places. Some of us refer to the country we live in to be our home. "I can't wait to get home after travelling in all these foreign countries where I don't know the customs, I don't speak the language, and I don't like the food." Others identify the church or religion to which they are affiliated as their home. "When I enter the Temple, I feel at home." "When I go to the Mosque, I have a sense of peace." "When I go to Mass, I feel I belong."

How much of our problems stem from our need to find a home outside of ourselves—a sense of place where we feel like we belong and are loved—instead of looking inward and connecting to forces outward? Some of the dictionary definitions for home are revealing:

1. A house, apartment, or other shelter that is the usual residence of a person, family, or household

2. The place in which one's domestic affections are centered
3. A dwelling place or retreat
4. The place or region where something is native or most common
5. Of, pertaining to, or connected with one's home or country; domestic
6. Principal or main
7. Reaching the mark aimed at
8. Deep, to the heart
9. Into the position desired
10. Toward its vessel
11. In a situation familiar to one; at ease
12. Having safely achieved one's goal

The definitions above demonstrate the range of feelings that the word "home" elicits. For me, the first half of the definitions refer to external places (e.g. house, region, country) and resonate less than the words that speak to a returning, that describe a subjective and internal experience, and that lead to a feeling of peace and stillness. Picking and choosing from the list of dictionary definitions, one might define HOME as "reaching the mark arrived at deep in the heart, which enables a person to feel familiar, safe, and at one."

I understand the appeal of different types of home. The house in which we were raised gives us a certain sense of home. It's where we return to after a day with friends, in school, or wherever we may go. Life partners can also bring a sense of peace and happiness and create a home of love and bonding. The hometown where we grew up grounds us in memories and gives us a sense of place. The home team for sports enthusiasts engenders a sense of loyalty, support, and rowdy displays of favoritism. The country in which we live and work gives us a sense of patriotism and obligation to serve in the defense of the homeland. The church to which people belong comforts them in hard times and challenges them to reach out and help others in good times. The core religious principles of faith, hope, and charity serve as bedrock principles for billions of people on earth. These are all good things. Our multiple homes give us a sense of security, pride, and belonging. It would be wrong to diminish the importance and purpose of these homes.

Indeed, I've been the beneficiary of several great homes. My parents were honest, decent, supportive, loving, and accepting people who always provided good food, comfortable space, and a few bucks for spending money now and then. I grew up in Plainwell, Michigan, a town that provided a solid education, winning sports teams, and a safe environment. I was raised as a Methodist and went to church with my family every Sunday. It seemed like a reasonable religious home for me at the time. Even though I didn't believe in the war, I still served my country in Vietnam and am supportive of protecting our homeland. America provided me with opportunities I could only have received in a few places in the world. It deserves my respect and patriotism.

The problem comes when we identify too strongly with any of these homes. If we over-identify with our nationality, our religion, our profession, our job, or even as a sports fan etc., it starts a vicious cycle. Identification leads to imagination (feelings of superiority or being more than what we are), which leads to negative emotion (when others don't share your beliefs, patriotism, home team fanaticism, etc.), which leads to bitterness, hatred, and violence. It's not difficult to find the end-points of this cycle.

Religions and nations have been very effective at marketing the idea of providing a home for people. Nietzsche would say that religions manipulate the masses for purposes of power and control. Others would say that religions reach out to what's best in people. Ironically, in my view, churches have been more constructive on a sociological and psychological level than they have been on a spiritual level.

In his poem "The Guest House," Rumi encourages us to be grateful for whatever comes. Perhaps that's the best way to visualize the desired end state for our subjective, internal HOME.

This being human is a guest house.
Every morning a new arrival.
A joy, a depression, a meanness, some momentary
awareness comes as an unexpected visitor.
Welcome and entertain them all!
Even if they are a crowd of sorrows, who violently sweep your
house empty of its furniture, still, treat each guest honorably.
He may be clearing you out for some new delight.
The dark thought, the shame, the malice.
Meet them at the door laughing and invite them in.
Be grateful for whatever comes. because each has been sent as
a guide from
beyond.

My aspiration for an internal HOME is to reach a state of being in which I am fully awake, unified, and conscious, even for fleeting moments. HOME is an acronym that describes that state:

I AM
>**H**ere
>>at **O**ne
>>>In the **M**oment
>>>>**E**ternally

"I AM" means the focus is on being vs. doing. When kids graduate from high school or college, I prefer to ask them, "Who are you going to be?" instead of "What are you going to do?" In *The Way of Life*, Lao Tzu says that the way to doing is being. Being can best be described as a state of calmness, equanimity, peace and stillness that manifests as our Presence and defines our Essence.

"Here" means being fully present. Not distracted by physical preoccupations. Not lost in emotional disappointments. Not thinking about some intellectual challenge or new idea. It means being where you are.

"At One" means seeing ourselves as an integral part of the whole. Connected to the Universe. Connected to each other. Understanding that all is one and one is all. Not focusing on differences. Appreciating commonalities. Having a visceral sense of peace.

"In the Moment" means being here now. Not fretting about what happened in the past. Not worrying about what might happen in the future. Not tweeting, texting, e-mailing, reading. Focused. Centered.

"Eternally" means forever. Time and space no longer matter. We are experiencing a perfect moment that extends throughout eternity.

It is a sense of immortality.

HOME is not discussed in terms of square feet, number of bathrooms, lot size, military might, economic power, athletic prowess, religious righteousness or grandeur of any kind. As such, there is no need for greed, envy, or feelings of superiority. It's simple. Ironically, building this HOME is much more difficult than building nations, palaces, or churches.

In short, the current state is that we are fighting the wrong wars in our life. We are more focused on the petty than the possible. We can assess our current state by observing how much time we spend reacting to petty issues outside ourselves and how much time we spend pursuing what's possible inside ourselves. Essentially, that assessment lets us know how we are doing on our spiritual growth. Are we making real efforts to grow or are we coasting through life with half-hearted attempts to increase our consciousness and to build our internal HOME? Instead of fighting wars about whose side some external God is on, I'm suggesting that the real war is confronting the challenges required to construct a virtual HOME within ourselves in entirely unconventional ways. We need to ask, "Are we fighting the right war or not?" Are we fighting with others about who is right, or are we fighting with ourselves to wake up and build our inner HOME?

In an attempt to figure all this out and find my HOME, I went to China for a month to study with a qigong master. I returned from China to many homes. I returned to America—a land I love. I came back to my family, the people who mean the most to me. I came back to my physical environment that I treasure. And yes, I came back a little more in touch with my internal HOME.

When I meditate and do qigong now, I try to connect with the Light, Warmth, and Love in the Universe. I imagine opening up to the stars, the Milky Way, the Universe, and to Infinity and try to bring all that positive energy into my body. Somehow the path from the universe to our inner HOME is littered with the debris of our cultural conditioning and personal experiences. Yet, when I look into the eyes of my baby grandchildren, I see unfiltered Light, Warmth, and Love. It's already there. And I wonder. What will happen to bring a shadow to that Light, to put a chill in that warmth, to turn that love into hate? What happens in peoples' lives that transform them from innocent and pure babies to dark, cold, and bitter adults? My observation is that they wander away from their HOME and their center in search of a different home away from themselves. Why is returning to the HOME that is already there fraught with so many obstacles?

The road from essence to personality is so much easier than the road from personality to essence. The road from substance to appearance is far more seductive than the road from appearance to substance.

Another Rumi poem captures the essence of this post.

Whoever Brought Me Here, Will Have To Take Me Home

"All day I think about it, then at night I say it. Where did I come from, and what am I supposed to be doing? I have no idea. My soul is from elsewhere, I'm sure of that, and I intend to end up there.

This drunkenness began in some other tavern. When I get back around to that place, I'll be completely sober. Meanwhile, I'm like a bird from another continent, sitting in this aviary. The day is coming when I fly off, but who is it now in my ear who hears my voice? Who says words with my mouth? Who looks out with my eyes? What is the soul? I cannot stop asking. If I could taste one sip of an answer, I could break out of this prison for drunks. I didn't come here of my own accord, and I can't leave that way. Whoever brought me here, will have to take me HOME. This poetry. I never know what I'm going to say. I don't plan it. When I'm outside the saying of it, I get very quiet and rarely speak at all"

Rumi raises the critical challenge, "if I could get a sip of an answer, I could break out of this prison for drunks."

This post simply describes my search for that elusive sip. It seems to me that the only way out is to go deep inside and work through. Only by great effort will be able to find our HOME.

As we try to find a way out of this prison for drunks, the idea is to increase the moments of peace, possibility, and connection in our lives. We need to realize there are always going to be intruders in our home. Accept them. Laugh at them. Come from a place of peace, possibility, and connection. That's all we can do on a personal level.

On a global level, Nationhood may be a necessary step along the way. The only real solution for lasting peace on our planet, however, is for people to build internal HOMES connected to the universe and to a nameless force and source.

Building a HOME means going deep.

So, be quiet.
Be still.
Be calm.
Be at peace.
Return to your true HOME

Our unruly I's will always raise their ugly heads. They are like snakes in the path of a horse. We lose all control. What's important is to stay committed to a continuing process and keep the faith that evolution and growth are possible.

Moving forward together, we need to find a community for our HOMES. A sense of connection is essential. Even though we try to power our individual homes with universal light, love, and warmth, we need to create a connected community as well in order to have a greater impact on this earth and to save the planet from climate change and nuclear disaster.

In conclusion, I believe that we need to find a HOME that gives us a sense of peace and a foundation for being more loving and responsible. I wrote this poem to summarize my point of view.

This HOME is not a fortress to protect your personality It is a place that frees your essence.

This HOME is not a building to defend your thoughts and beliefs. It is an inner warmth that has no fence.

This HOME is not an external place to give you a sense of order. It is an internal launching pad to release your energy beyond any border.

This HOME is not a retreat to make you feel selected. It is a simple sensibility that enables you to feel connected.

At a minimum, consciousness and awareness are good things independent of any transcendent possibilities. Being aware means we have few blind spots, some level of sensitivity to others, and a feeling of being alive and awake for our brief period on this earth. At a maximum, being conscious means we develop a crystalized essence; a connection to higher energies; a Oneness with the Absolute; a higher probability for another chance; an enlightened state; an evolutionary advance; an ultimate liberation from the trials of this world; a greater appreciation for what's unfolding in front of us, a feeling of freedom from our habits, limitations, and constricting beliefs, a deeper and richer understanding of possibility; a sense of unification; and a more powerful ability to heal with the light, love, and warmth of the universe.

And death becomes just another moment.

May you find your HOME and be at peace. May we find a way to dance all the way to death. And, together, may we find a way to join with each other as one community on earth dedicated to the preservation of the planet and to the generation of new possibilities for all.

I can't think of a better way to end this post and this chapter, than sharing some lyrics of one of my favorite songs by Leonard Cohen, *Dance Me to the End of Love*. If there is anyone who is at HOME in the Universe, it is this wonderful songwriter and poet.

Dance me to your beauty with a burning violin
Dance me through the panic 'til I'm gathered safely in
Lift me like an olive branch and be my homeward dove
Dance me to the end of love

Organizational Health

The primary purpose of my work with organizations has been to create humane, innovative, and productive work environments. What I learned after working with more than 200 organizations world-wide over the course of 30 years is that the fundamental building block of a healthy organization is trust.

Just as trust has been destroyed in many communities between ethnic groups and the police, trust can also be destroyed in organizations where the leaders have no street CRED – Credibility, Relationships, Ego-Management, and Dependability. Their words are empty (no credibility), their relationships are demeaning, they are perceived as abusing their power (Ego-Management), and their actions are unreliable (Dependability). That is why I chose the post on Building Trust as the lead article for this chapter. None of the other posts matter if there is no trust.

With a high level of trust in organizations and an absence of fear, however, it is possible to create organizational soul; engage, energize and inspire employees to mobilize behind meaningful work; unleash potential; engender positivity; develop capabilities; foster creative thinking, and reflect on possibilities. These are the topics I've tried to explore in this chapter.

Since our jobs consume so much of our time, it's critical to create environments that support balance, mindfulness, and purposeful work. If our work degenerates into a soul-sucking, spirit-deleting experience, what hope do we have of becoming conscious, spiritual beings? Work matters.

Building Trust

Trust is the foundational building block for organizational health. Just as diet and exercise are the key starting points for physical health, trust is the "must have" for building a healthy, productive, and innovative work environment. Without trust, you have no chance of creating the kind of organizational culture you may want to build.

Trust has two components: individual and institutional. Individual trust is defined as a firm belief in the reliability, truth, ability, or strength of someone or something. Institutional trust is defined as the confidence that others will act as we expect. Some institutional trust theories stress the role of networks and relationship among people and others emphasize the importance of shared norms. Trust is based on an assessment of the competence, integrity, and benevolence of individuals and institutions.

Individual trust can be built through four factors: credibility, relationship-building, ego-management, and dependability (CRED). Credibility is all about words. Individuals with high credibility are known for doing rigorous research, having deep expertise and broad experience, and making evidence based decisions based on thorough analysis. Highly credible people are authentic – they talk straight.

Relationships are built through empathy and transparency. People-oriented individuals build strong personal connections by making the effort to reach out; actively inquiring about others' interests, values, aspirations, and dreams; demonstrating understanding about how people are thinking and feeling; sharing perspective; and being appropriately transparent and self-disclosing.

Individuals who are able to manage their egos are perceived as being genuinely helpful, actively seeking ways to help others succeed, and not being overly self-promoting. Ego management means being more like Mother Theresa and less like Donald Trump.

Dependability is all about actions. Highly dependable people do what they say when they say they are going to do it. They are perceived as reliable, consistent, predictable, conscientious, loyal, and responsible. A helpful exercise for assessing your individual trustworthiness is to rate each of these four factors on a scale of 1-10 with 1 being low and 10 being high. Complete the following grid and compute your CRED score by assessing how you rate yourself, how you rate one of your colleagues, and how you think that colleague would rate you.

CRED Factors:	Self Rating	Your rating of a colleague	Colleague's rating of you
Credibility			
Relationship-Building			
Ego-Management			
Dependability			
Total			

Institutional trust can be built through four mechanisms: legal provisions, reputation, certifications, and community norms and structures. Legal provisions can improve trust when they enable consistent compliance with internal and external policies and regulations and by clear and fair employment contracts. Reputation contributes to trust when it is built by the social responsibility it displays in the communities in which it lives and by its response to mistakes or product deficiencies. For example, J&J increased its brand value as a trusted drug supplier by responding aggressively to the tampering of Tylenol bottles. GM, on the other hand, tarnished its reputation by the recent revelations that it covered up ignition switch defects and failed to take steps to fix the problem even though the costs were very low. Certifications can also increase institutional trust for groups such as Doctors and lawyers and by the number of employees who come from elite universities. McKinsey, for example, prides itself in hiring from Ivy League schools and leverages those pedigrees to create trust among its clients. It's the community norms and structures, however, on which I want to focus in this article. These represent the desired values and behaviors in an organization that, in my mind, yield the highest return of all the options for building institutional trust.

Healthy organizations create and abide by values that engender institutional trust. The most common values organizations publish on building walls and in annual reports are: respect, integrity, interdependence, innovation, and quality. The question is, are those values dead or alive in the organization? Institutional trust can be measured by analyzing the gap between stated values and day-to-day behaviors – how things really work "around here." When the gaps are small, institutional trust is high. When gaps are large, institutional trust is low. Organizations can create values, norms, and behaviors that come alive in organizations by involving employees in the development of the values, by periodically auditing the values, and by forming task forces to look at ways to close the gaps. A task force needs to be formed by the executive committee and its reports and recommendations need to be taken seriously. I have always recommended referring to this task force as a soul committee whose sole responsibility is to calibrate the gaps between stated values and actual behaviors. I have found few organizations who are willing to embrace that idea.

Patrick Lencioni has written several books which posit that trust is the basic building block for functional teams and organizations. With trust, it is possible to engage in healthy conflict, inspire commitment, hold people accountable, and achieve great results. Without trust, conflict goes underground, commitment shrinks, accountability disappears, and results suck. These all seem like good reasons to build individual and institutional trust. Why haven't we?

Corporate Spirit:
Oxymoron or Possibility

Spirituality is coming to the workplace thinly veiled as mindfulness, awareness, and stress management. As the veil gets lifted, the questions arise: does it belong, can it co-exist with profitability, and what are the dangers?

Does spirituality belong in the workplace? It depends. If spirituality is defined in terms such as connectedness, community, and joy; then the answer is yes. If spirituality is defined in religious terms, then the answer is no.

A primary requirement of leadership is being self-aware or connected to yourself. A primary requirement of high performing teams is a sense of connection with each other. A primary requirement for motivation is being connected to a higher purpose. Thus, to the extent that spirituality builds connectedness, it would seem that it can play a vital role in organizational life.

Community is also a central facet of healthy organizations. There are communities of interest, communities of practice, and a palpable sense of community within high performing organizations. Therefore, if spirituality can help to build community then it must belong.

Finally, recent studies show that employees are much happier and motivated if they believe their work contributes to helping others. Thus, if spirituality can give people a sense of mission beyond themselves, it would seem that it belongs in the workplace.

On the other hand, if spirituality is cast in religious terms, then it is problematic. Just as there are clear constitutional guidelines for the separation of church and state, there are also clear dangers of imposing ideology in the workplace. Organizations should not be seen as "ripe for harvest" among religious zealots or evangelicals.

Over 30 years ago, I introduced the idea of teaching connectedness at Johnson & Johnson as a part of their wellness program and as a way of introducing spirituality in the workplace. They didn't embrace it at the time, but the book I wrote on *Connectedness* is now a critical part of the psychiatric rehab program at Boston University. I also included a chapter on Connectedness in my book on The *Complete Guide to Wellness* because it complemented physical, emotional, and mental health with spiritual health.

In 2001, Julie Meek and I published the book, *Spiritual Leadership*, which discusses how to transform dysfunctional organizations into healthy communities. It documents the work of several "soul models" who created healthy communities in their respective workplaces.

To come back to the title of this piece, *Corporate Spirit: an Oxymoron or a Possibility*, I clearly vote for the latter. I believe spirituality belongs in the workplace as long as it transparently relates to creating community, connectedness, meaning, and moments of joy and is not a mask for religious indoctrination.

In this scientific age, the pendulum has swung too far in the direction of objective, quantitative analysis at the expense of qualitative, subjective analysis. Ken Wilbur has written an excellent book, *Integral Psychology,* which brilliantly addresses this shift. He argues for an all quadrant, all level approach - which simply means that you take into account spirit and soul as well as body and mind, and that you take into account qualitative and subjective as well as quantitative and objective. One does not deny the other. It is a mistake to go "all-in" on one way or the other. Introducing spirituality in the workplace does not mean you are anti-scientific. It should be quite the opposite – you are finding ways of integrating science and spirituality.

Creating Organizational Soul

After publishing <u>Corporate Culture Change</u>, <u>The Culture Change Sourcebook</u>, and <u>Ethical Leadership</u> in the late 1980's, I was retained by Lotus Development Corporation in Cambridge, Massachusetts to help them align their culture behind a new network-centric strategy to better differentiate their company from it's arch-rival Microsoft. Since Microsoft owned the proprietary operating system required for running almost all applications at the time and had developed the Office suite of products that all worked together, it dominated the software market. Lotus could only compete by creating a new space and by becoming the preferred partner for a world-wide network of value-added vendors. Microsoft's proclamation that it wanted to dominate the world did not make people want to jump in bed with them if they could avoid it. Culture, therefore, played a major role in Lotus's success.

The history is a vital part of this story. When Bill Gates founded Microsoft in 1975, he was not known as the kind and generous, philanthropic benefactor that he is now after establishing the Gates Foundation and donating $40 billion of his personal wealth. In the early days of the software wars, he was notorious for working 20 hours a day and biting people's heads off for being less than brilliant in the brief time he begrudgingly gave them. Evidently, he and Steve Jobs were taking the same anger pills. He clearly hadn't discovered meditation and massage or asked gurus to help him become an enlightened leader. While he has mellowed over time and has become one of the most benevolent givers in history, he wasn't always so kind and gentle. But back to the main story.

In order to ensure that it's culture was not only aligned with its new strategy, but also retained its most important clients, Lotus established a Soul Committee whose sole purpose was to ensure that day-to-day behaviors were congruent with the lofty operating principles and core values they had created with great care and diligence. I was asked to serve as the consultant to the Soul Committee. As a result of that work and the increasing awareness of the power of culture on human development and organizational success, I decided to write the book *Creating Organizational Soul – the Source of Positive Change and Transformation.*

My path to that decision took a rather circuitous route with multiple potholes along the way. A year in Vietnam rocked my perception of the world and how it works. Eight years in jail working with inmates and delinquents opened my eyes to the ways in which the environment influences peoples' lives. Four years working with drug abusers, teen-age pregnant girls, and social service organizations deepened my appreciation for how hard life can be for folks. Two years working in hospitals put me face to face with the results of living in an unhealthy culture and practicing unhealthy behaviors. Two years in an elementary school gave me a better understanding of how classroom environments established by variety of teachers can produce positive or negative outcomes for kids. And twenty years working with leaders of the largest corporations in the world broadened my perspective on the relationship between healthy organizations and healthy people. In short, I found that soulful organizations make people healthy, happy and productive, while soulless organizations suck the life and energy out of people. And, just to be clear, soulful organizations are more profitable in the long run.

Based on that hodgepodge of experience, I identified the seven principles of soulful organizations.

1. If every interaction, day after day, is viewed as an opportunity to create a meaningful work environment (humane, innovative, productive, and fun), the possibilities for organizational soul will take root.
2. When words and actions are congruent, people are more motivated.
3. When people feel good about what they are doing, productivity improves.
4. When people are aligned with a larger purpose, passion develops.
5. When customers experience an organization's commitment to help, partnerships develop and trust builds.
6. When people are continually thinking about what's possible, innovation increases.
7. If an organization creates a soul, it's stakeholders will grow – and so will it.

If the idea of organizational soul still seems a little soft and fuzzy to you, here are some examples from a variety of organizations that might change your perception.

<u>Google</u>: "When I entered Google for the first time, I immediately caught a whiff of a culture that was distinct from any that I had experienced before. I saw many of the

things I'd read about in the countless articles about Google and its culture. As I waited in the lobby for my host, I watched young hipsters in jeans flying through the halls on scooters. Through the glass doors, I could see people in conference rooms sitting on fat, brightly colored exercise balls as they intensely discussed issues during a video-conference. And as we walked to the interview room, we passed brightly lit micro-kitchens stocked with countless types of organic juices and bowls of fruit, and lined with gins full of nuts, cereal, crackers, and cookies – an indication of just one of Google's most famous perks: free food. More interesting than the cool accoutrements, however, was the energy that filled the air at Google. There was a palpable sense that things were happening. The people in the hall wore expressions of thoughtfulness and intensity, rather than the typical corporate haggardness that pervades the cube farms of many of the companies I'd worked with in the past." Jesse Haines, Google Executive

Homeless Solutions: "I think of soul as the heart of the organization – those ways of being that make an organization alive and passionate about the work. I think of the energy, imagination, and creativity that one brings to work and the desire to make the many tasks of the work add up to the climax of success and achievement. Somehow, soul, life breath, and life-force work together. The justice orientation of our goals is that of making life and lives better, creating systems that are responsible and responsive, inviting all players to think, act, and lead for the good of all. How do we create soul at Homeless Solutions? I think it is by being drawn into the notion of acting justly, doing justice, and being fair to others and ourselves. I suspect it has to do with wanting the best for people around us, including the clients, tenants, and the (homeless) guests on whose behalf we work. Also, we demonstrate respect and care for our donors. Without their support, help, and energy, we could not be the vehicle for bringing help. I imagine it has to do with treating others as we want to be treated. Always looking for ways to stop and reach out to each other in genuine care." Dr. Betsey Hall, CEO, Homeless Solutions.

<u>Berkeley-Carroll Elementary School, Brooklyn, NY</u>: When you enter a classroom with soul, children will look happy and engaged. They will greet you with a handshake and a smile, and they will look you in the eye. They realize they are ambassadors for the room, and they feel proud to show you around and introduce you to the learning and tradition that occur every day inside their room. A classroom with soul is a powerful place of intellectual and emotional growth. Every child feels certain he has a place, that he is important, and that his job is valuable. A soulful classroom doesn't occur by accident, however. It happens through the daily activities, rituals, and traditions that a teacher builds into the children's day. In my classroom, and many others in my school, I use an approach called "The Responsive Classroom" to build community, interdependence, and accountability into my room. Every morning, students in my classroom are greeted with a message that compliments their hard work from earlier in the week and forecasts upcoming events, activities, and projects. "Good Morning Powerful Readers" the message might read, or "Hello Mighty Mathematicians!" or "Good Morning Cooperative Classmates." Every morning, they remember how powerful, smart, thoughtful, and eager they are. They are reminded that their hard work, focus, energy, and cooperation is valued and expected." Rebecca Bellingham, Instructor, Columbia Teachers College.

Whether it's a for-profit corporation, a not-for-profit social service organization, or a school, you know an organization has soul when you hear people saying:

- We trust each other
- We feel empowered
- We engage in meaningful dialogue
- There is a high level of reflection on critical issues
- We engage in healthy, non-violent conflict
- We are passionate about a higher purpose
- There is a high level of creative energy
- We are inclusive
- We are always learning
- We are caring and compassionate
- There is a high level of integrity
- We value and respect differences
- We are genuine
- We are brutally honest about the facts of our situation
- We encourage growth and well-being
- We seek ways to help each other succeed
- We collaborate
- We hold each other accountable
- We drive for results
- We are open, honest, and direct

These norms and values just don't happen without leadership role modeling and support. Leaders must demonstrate these norms and behaviors and design reward systems to reinforce them.

I believe our purpose in life is to develop our souls as individuals and as organizations. As individuals, we have been given the gift of possibility – the opportunity to take a spark of life and grow it into something useful. As organizations, the same possibility exists. In each moment, day-to-day, we either make a positive difference or we don't. We are either open to letting positive energy work in wondrous ways or we are not.

Exploitation Masquerading as Engagement

Most companies measure employee engagement. It represents one critical way to determine the level of commitment and productivity of their human capital. An abundance of research suggests a high correlation between employee engagement and great performance. Engagement is typically defined as "the willingness to invest discretionary effort at work – to go above and beyond what's expected. In a recent New York Times article, Tony Schwartz, the CEO of Life@ Work, admits that the book he wrote over a decade ago, *The Power of Full Engagement*, is in need of a major revision. He suggests that engagement has morphed into burnout and exploitation.

After a major research study in 2012, Towers Perrin found that high engagement, as it has been traditionally defined, is no longer sufficient to achieve high performance. The study determined that employees in companies with the highest profits were sustainably engaged which describes how employees feel when their companies promote their physical, emotional, and social well-being. Their study corroborates the results of earlier studies on employee commitment, i.e. high performing employees believe that their leaders care about their well-being, are able to achieve a reasonable balance between work and personal life, and report a manageable level of stress in their life.

Over the past 40 years, I have worked with hundreds of organizations. All of them have struggled with these three critical issues: how to promote employee well-being, how to allow for work/life balance, and how to help employees manage stress, while simultaneously beating Wall Street expectations. Unfortunately, in the last decade, I have noticed stress going up, care for employee well-being going down, and balance going by the wayside. In many companies with whom I currently consult, employees regularly work 60-70 hours per week under tight deadlines and demanding conditions. Result: stress up, care down, and balance out. The question is, "at what point does "engagement turn into exploitation?"

What I have found to be helpful to organizations, who really don't want to cross the line from engagement to exploitation, is have a scale to measure where they are and to point to where they want to be. The scale I use for employee motivation and productivity is:

5.0: Inspired
4.0: Energized
3.0: Sustainably Engaged
2.0: Committed
1.0: Satisfied

Here's a brief description of each level.

<u>Satisfaction</u>: It's a good thing when employees are satisfied with their compensation, benefits, and working conditions. The problem is that satisfaction doesn't always translate into commitment. A satisfied employee is one who does what is asked and nothing more. Satisfaction can also turn quickly

into complacency, and a satisfied employee is usually only one complaint away from being dissatisfied.

Commitment: A committed employee not only does what is asked, but also applies him or herself fully to the task at hand. A committed employee clarifies requirements for every task and applies the right capabilities to meet those requirements.

Sustainable Engagement: A sustainably engaged employee participates fully in decisions effecting work and takes full responsibility for completing tasks on time in accordance with requirements. Engaged employees feel informed of what's going on and involved in decisions that affect them. By definition, the sustainably engaged employee is able to achieve performance objectives AND work/life balance.

Energized: An energized employee brings fresh ideas to projects, adds value to others, and contributes to product/process improvement. It's impossible to have an energized employee with no fuel in the tank. Energized employees are not only getting time to rest, reflect, and re-charge, they are also looking for opportunities to lead and make a difference. In order to energize employees, the organization must create a culture that supports multi-dimensional needs.

Inspiration: An inspired employee finds joy in his relationships at work and in the contribution he or she is making to the larger good. At this level the employee needs to believe in the mission of the organization and feel that the work is meaningful and impactful.

So what is required to achieve each level of motivation and productivity? The chart below summarizes the key factors:

Level of Motivation and Productivity	Key Requirements to achieve this level
5.0: Inspired	Meaningful purpose and mission
4.0: Energized	Positive and supportive culture
3.0: Sustainably engaged	Genuine, responsive, caring leadership
2.0: Committed	Clear objectives and developmental opportunities
1.0: Satisfied	Fair pay, benefits, and expectations

The challenge for most organizations today is to inspire and energize their employees while maintaining a competitive advantage in the global marketplace. Engagement is a good place to start, but it can't cross the line and slip into exploitation. If you are an employee, where do you rate yourself on this scale? If you are an organizational leader, are you creating the conditions that fulfill the requirements to achieve the level of motivation and productivity you profess to desire. How do you know when you've crossed the line from engagement to exploitation?

Labels Limits, and Levels

Dr. Bill Anthony, the highly respected, world-renowned, executive director of the Psychiatric Rehabilitation Center at Boston University, initiated classes with new students by throwing the DSM (Diagnostic and Statistical Manual of Mental Disorders) into the waste basket. This dramatic statement was intended to communicate to people entering the mental health field that labels limit our ability to see the potential and possibilities of another human being. People with mental or physical challenges are too easily dismissed or discarded by whatever diagnosis is assigned to them. They too easily become a "case" instead of a person with challenges with whom we can connect on multiple levels and help in multiple ways.

Labels are a convenient way to place limits on what others can do, think, feel, or experience. This phenomenon plays out in our individual lives, in our classrooms, in our organizations, and at the United Nations on the most complex social, economic, and political issues. It seems that we are more prone to label and limit than we are to explore potential levels of development, change, and growth.

In mental health organizations, we label people by their diagnosis. In geo-political conflicts, we label people by their religion. We assign the characteristics of individuals to the groups to which they allegedly belong whether that is Muslim, Jewish, Christian, Hindu, or Buddhist. In education, we label people by their IQ scores or diagnostic category. In social disruptions and deliberations, we label people by their race, sexual orientation, or gender. All of these labels limit our ability to see what's possible if we were willing and able to elevate our discussions to higher levels of thinking and relating.

In his classrooms, Dr. Anthony didn't stop at the dramatic gesture, he always went on to encourage students to look at the possibilities of the people they were supposed to be helping and to look for links to other social agencies that could assist their growth and development. As a result of his efforts and the contributions of his staff, The Center for Psychiatric Rehab has been recognized for many years as the premier provider of mental health solutions, as the trusted advisor to clients and agencies, and as the exemplar for establishing a whole new level of service in the helping profession.

When I talk about higher levels, I am talking about the ability to frame any discussion around a range of possible interventions and outcomes. In the 50 years I have spent working in military organizations, educational institutions, health care systems, and corporate environments, I have seen a wide range of interventions and outcomes. Some amazing interventions resulted in incredible outcomes. Any many others smelled pretty ordinary. Here are a few examples of the lesser sort.

I've listened to Harvard Professors talk about change. Most of their highly articulate elucidations are at the conceptual level – level 2. We can measure the level of educational discourse on this scale:

5.0: Teachable skills
4.0: Personalized objectives
3.0: Meaningful principles
2.0: Clarifying concepts
1.0: Edifying facts

It's not that facts, concepts, and principles are bad. - quite the contrary. We need a strong base of knowledge on which we can build, but if concepts don't translate into principles, objectives, and skills, then real change won't happen.

I've observed leadership development programs in the leading corporations. Most of the fancy PowerPoint presentations and aesthetically pleasing learning materials are not only conceptual, but they also don't adequately address the critical needs of their organizations, e.g. how to become more interdependent, how to inspire employees to choose to be optimally motivated, how to position themselves in a changing marketplace, how to align all of their capabilities behind their vision and mission, how to become trusted advisors to their customers, how to process constantly changing conditions and standards, etc. There are also scales to measure the level of discourse on organizational issues:

Levels of employee feelings, i.e. how people feel about working for a particular leader:

5.0: Inspired
4.0: Invested
3.0: Involved
2.0: Informed
1.0: Ignored

Levels of team behavior:

5.0: Interdependent
4.0: Collaborative
3.0: Independent
2.0: Competitive
1.0: Dependent

Levels of customer relationships:

5.0: Trusted Advisor
4.0: Valued Added Partner
3.0: Solution Provider
2.0: Services Vendor
1.0: Product Pusher

In most organizations, employees feel informed, are committed to their tasks, are competitive with each other for pay raises and promotions, and sell some variety of product or service. In short, most organizational life takes place at level 2 – not a particularly healthy state.

I've heard politicians talk about change we can believe in. Most of the pandering is based on opinion polls designed to secure a majority at elections. Wouldn't it be refreshing to hear politicians engaged in an elevated conversation about saving the planet and enhancing life on it. As a case in point, governments have been talking about world peace ever since we first experienced the horrors of war. Why is this elusive goal so difficult to achieve? Why is transformation so difficult? We have lofty ideals, but reality keeps pulling us into the muck. We hear all the words, but we don't see results.

Here is scale to measure the discourse on politics.

5.0: Promoting Peace
4.0: Producing Programs
3.0: Planning
2.0: Promising and Pretending
1.0: Pandering to what people want to hear

So, why is it we aren't seeing the changes we keep hearing about in our classrooms, in our organizations, and in governments around the world? The reason is simple. All of the conversations are stuck at level 1 or level 2, and there is great resistance to moving up the scale. Why, you might ask again? Because level 1 and level 2 not only require less effort, there are more material and psychic rewards at those levels.

But let's take this conversation out of the sky and onto the ground to a more personal experience. Scales can be used to explore levels of functioning at the individual level as well. It is possible to assess our own levels of functioning and to ask what might be possible with a bit more effort and what 'real' rewards might be available to us at the higher levels.

You can do your own assessment or even create your own scales. The important step is to take an honest, objective, and impartial assessment of your level of functioning in all dimensions of your life and to make the effort to move up whatever scales you adapt and adopt. And the key question to ask is, "How do I move from labels that limit to levels that elevate?"

I wish I knew how to convince people to focus on levels instead of labels. I wonder what would happen if conversations changed to how we move up the scales based on an accurate assessment of where we are, and on a realistic assessment of where we need to be. I wish I were engaged in more conversations about how we can move up the scales. They don't need to be the same scales I listed above. You can create your own scales that are meaningful to you. Just create something more aspirational than acquiring material wealth and/or stroking your ego.

I don't have a DSM manual to throw in the waste basket to get your attention. All I can do is to keep throwing my thoughts out to the universe in the hope that people find them useful. I can't stop people from labeling and limiting, but I can suggest scales that could change the conversation. And I can continue to stay engaged with the exceptionally talented and committed people I know who are actively initiating creative ways to help all of us move up the scales.

Selection of Coaches

Forty years ago, I wrote my doctoral dissertation on the selection of counselors for public high schools. I didn't write it to create a career-defining, landmark study. I wrote it to check off a box for the completion of my doctoral degree in counseling psychology. Little did I know that the profession of coaching and counseling would explode in the next century. Now, practically everyone either has a coach or is a coach. The question is, how do you select a good coach if you want one? How do you know which coach is right for you.

As it turns out, the heaviest consumers of coaches are professional athletes and corporate executives. Clearly, Tiger Woods would have been better off selecting a life coach rather than a golf coach. He was getting advice on swinging, but apparently he was mis-applying the concepts in his personal life. And many organizations have hired coaches to improve leadership impact and organizational health.

As I was reflecting on my dissertation at dinner with my younger daughter and her significant other (he asked what my dissertation was), I realized that the provocative position I took four decades ago had more relevance today than it did when I wrote it.

Since I know you can bear the suspense no longer, I will share my conclusions. Essentially, I suggested that choosing counselors required an assessment of their physical, intellectual, emotional, and spiritual levels of functioning.

My outrageous proposal was to line them up and have a push up contest. You may dismiss this idea as preposterously silly, but there was a logic to my thinking as well as a rebellious spirit driving it. Yes, I know, this would have never flown at Harvard. Well, that's Harvard's problem – a topic I will discuss in another post.

So here's the logic. The easiest dimension to change in our lives is the physical dimension. As one of my mentors once said, "if you can't change your physical functioning, what are you going to change – your underwear?" So, if I'm going to select a coach of any variety (life coach, sports coach, career coach, executive coach, spiritual coach), I will want to know how well they take care of the physical dimension of their life. What is their level of fitness? Are they flexible enough to handle changes in appointments? Do they have enough endurance to listen to my endless whining? Can they bring the intensity required to handle big moments? Please note that I'm not proposing that every coach or counselor should be an elite athlete. I'm just suggesting that someone dispensing advise on how to live your life ought to be attending to their own most basic dimension.

A coach should also be functioning at an acceptable intellectual level. Personally, I don't' want to pay someone to ask me a series of stupid questions. I want a coach to be well-read, informed about a wide variety of topics, and able to ask provocative questions that will enable me to think about my issues in a new light and in a new frame. Growing intellectually is the second most difficult challenge of human development. You have to read, inquire, analyze, synthesize, and innovate. I don't see much value in a coach who can't identify themes, patterns, and underlying motivations.

An effective coach needs to function at high levels emotionally. I want a coach who has done the work to explore who they are and why they are who they are. I want someone who has not only gone down and in, but has come up and out. I want someone who has taken a hard look at the past and has a bright view of the future. I want someone who can not only identify accurately their own feelings and values, but also can also penetrate the depth of my feelings and what's most important to me. I don't want sympathy, and I don't want to hear, "that's nice, I understand, I hear you, Ummmm, or Ahhhh. I want to hear, for example, "you feel excited by your possibilities because you have a range of options available to you."

Perhaps most importantly, an effective coach has to function at high levels spiritually. This forth dimension is the most difficult, but it is the most powerful. I want someone who understands alienation and connection, someone who understands loneliness and community, someone who understands despair and joy, someone who can relate to negativity and positivity. A highly evolved spiritual coach exudes energy and life. This person has done the work and has made the effort to master disciplines such as Yoga, QiGong, Pranic Healing, etc. This person is a source of love, light, and power. I want someone who is attuned to the essence of life and who knows how to activate and align my own energy. I have been fortunate to have several of these people in my life.

Unfortunately, most of the coaches I have seen in my long career can't even pass the first test, much less the second, third, or fourth. Yes, they have their certifications. They know how to ask stupid questions and evoke sympathetic utterances. But my question is, who certifies the certifiers? I have seen the products of multiple certification programs, and very few are able to meet the basic criteria set forth above. And yet, the demand continues to grow. Why is that?

Primarily, the field is growing because it is satisfying what clients want. And they don't want much. It is possible to scale what consumers of coaching services want. This scale, originally articulated by my friend and colleague Dr. Bill Obrien (the best executive coach I know), explains why there are so many coaches and so many satisfied clients.

    5.0: Perform
    4.0: Produce
    3.0: Position
    2.0: Pamper
    1.0: Pout

At level one, clients simply want to pout and complain about their situation. They don't want to be pushed or challenged. There are many coaches who are perfectly willing an able to hand out Kleenex, sympathize, and ask questions that prime the flow of negativity, self pity, and self justification.

At level two, clients want to be pampered. They want unconditional love and a supportive ear. There are many coaches who are very good at stroking egos and nurturing self-esteem. In fact, they are in high demand.

At level three, clients want to position themselves for larger roles in their respective organizations. Positioning is an acceptable goal for clients. They want to learn how to develop and promote their brand, heighten visibility, build social networks, and develop relationships with mentors or advocates who can advance their career. There are many coaches who can respond accurately to feelings and meaning and help their clients achieve their career aspirations.

At level four, clients want to produce better outcomes in their lives and in their work. They want their coach to ask tough questions and to suggest ways to modify their leadership behaviors in order to create highly energized and engaged teams. There are a few coaches who have the perspective to offer meaningful advice, who can personalize goals, and who are willing to take the risk of speaking truth to power.

At level five, clients want to perform at optimal levels and realize their possibilities. They want to grow physically, intellectually, emotionally, and spiritually in order to live better, learn better, and work better. And they are willing to make the effort and pay the price. Clients whose goal is high performance are open to new ways of thinking, they are seeking ways to help others succeed, and they are dedicated to creating a work environment in which passionate people choose to be optimally motivated. I know a handful of coaches who are able to achieve that level of functioning. If you are lucky enough to find one, hire him or her immediately. But first ask, what do I really want from this coaching process.

Dusting off the dissertation didn't make me want to go back and start a new academic career in the theory of selection. It simply reminded me that some ideas have lasting value even if they, at first, appear to be outrageous.

Step Back

In 2013, Sheryl Sandberg's *Lean In* became a massive cultural phenomenon, and its title became an instant catchphrase for empowering women. The book soared to the top of best-seller lists both nationally and internationally, igniting global conversations about women and ambition. Sandberg packed theaters, dominated op-ed pages, appeared on every major television show and on the cover of *Time* magazine, and sparked ferocious debate about women and leadership. She made the point that success in organizational life meant leaning into an issue and making your voice heard.

While her general principle applies to everyone who wants to "succeed" or "win" the race to the top, there may be an unintended consequence of too much leaning in and too little stepping back. I was reminded of that phenomenon when I read Dick Cavett's op-ed in the New York Times yesterday (April 25, 2015). He reminded us how hard it was to go back to Vietnam and remember the angst and agony of that time. He recalled asking Kissinger how he would respond to a father who asked, "was this war worth the loss of my son? Kissinger evaded the question by blaming the Kennedy administration for the war. Leaning into Vietnam, Iraq, Afghanistan, Libya, Syria, and who knows what next, can be summarized as a bunch of self-serving idiots engaging in magical thinking and then numbing themselves to the consequences of their stupid decisions while refusing to take ownership when the whole thing implodes. In war, leaning in (unleashing torrents of bombs and sending unending lines of poor kids without other options into suicidal missions) usually results in ill-conceived decisions to exercise our military might to create irreconcilable conflicts. Stepping back and considering alternative possibilities might well lead to more sustainable, more humane, and less violent solutions. If only we could have found the courage to step back in Vietnam before leaning in.

The value of stepping back not only applies to military interventions; it also applies to every aspect of individual and organizational life. What does it mean to step back? Quite simply, it means stopping long enough to take a deep breath. As my daughter says, there is power in the pause. It means taking time to reflect on all the values inherent in any consequential decision. It requires us to get out of the flow of any current that is pushing us to a particular destination, and step back from the edge long enough to survey the scenery and ask ourselves the hard questions. Is this a river of my choosing, or was I thrown-in by some external force? Is this river taking me where I want to go, or might I be racing hell-bent for a swamp? Is there any thing I could do or learn that would help me navigate this flow? What impact is this raging river having on the communities it runs through? Where is the higher ground? These are the questions we ask when we step back.

It's hard to give due consideration to those questions or, for that matter, contemplate, meditate, or cogitate effectively when we are being swept through the rapids hanging on for dear life. Stepping back from the bank helps us secure solid footing and a sense of being grounded.

Life, in most organizations, is like riding a raft through intense rapids without a life jacket. What helps is having a leader you trust and co-workers you like and respect. Great teams take time for introspection, reflection, and renewal. These teams usually enjoy a glorious, fun-filled ride to the ocean. Because all members of great teams actively seek ways to help each other succeed, they form deep connections and find real joy in working together as a community. Dysfunctional teams usually make mad rushes to achieve quarterly milestones, which in the end, they miss. These teams suffer through exhausting, stressful ordeals and end up crashing on the rocks. Some people on those teams may survive by leaning in, but others fail or fall out of the raft. So, what's the difference between great teams and dysfunctional teams? For me, the biggest difference is that great teams take time to step back and take a hard look at where they are, where they need to be, and how they plan to get there together. They have clearly defined, and commonly held views of their vision, values, purpose, and mission. Specifically, they have clear means of measuring success.

In my experience, great teams measure REAL success on these four criteria:

1. All systems are integrated and interdependent, all decisions are evidence-based, and all hierarchies are designed for inclusiveness – not exclusiveness.
2. Everyone is dedicated to creating experiences that foster growth and community.
3. Everyone feels connected to each other and to the vision, values, mission, and purpose.
4. Everyone owns responsibility for their actions and leverages all experiences – good and bad – for learning and contributing to the greater good.

In order to accomplish those goals, however, teams need to step back and take a hard look at their organizational culture and their individual behavior. In most cases, that means acknowledging four ugly realities:

1. We engage in magical and mythological thinking.
2. We are more concerned with profits and pride than relationships, community, and transformational experiences.
3. We go through most days asleep or dreaming – armored and numb.
4. We disown, self-justify, or repress our bad behavior or experiences.

Clearly, there are big gaps between where great teams want to be and where most teams really exist. It's impossible to bridge those gaps while you are being swept down a racing stream of profit maximization and self promotion. It is imperative to step back and commit to the strategies required to achieve real success. If you still want to Lean In, that's your choice. And you may "succeed" in the apparent world. But if you want REAL success in the REAL world, then follow these four steps: Lean back. Reach Back. Reach In. Step back.

Leadership

Organizational health is dependent on strong leadership. This chapter summarizes the books I have written on the topic based on my experiences teaching leadership development from Mom and Pop shops to Fortune 100 companies.

Just as I chose "Building Trust" as the lead article for the chapter on Organizational Health, I chose "Ethical Leadership" as the opening article for this chapter. Before you can discuss competency requirements for leadership, it is necessary to discuss the character requirements of effective leaders.

After addressing the character and competency requirements of leadership, this chapter address the myths and realities of leadership, and some generic qualities of great leaders depending upon the requirements of the situation. Exemplary leaders from Jesus to Jane Adams are discussed.

Ethical Leadership

In 1987, Barry Cohen and I wrote the book, *Ethical Leadership*. We published the first version of the book when greed was still in its relative infancy and millionaires (much less billionaires) were still relatively rare. It thus preceded the economic boom of the 1990s, a decade in which market values escalated to what was then outrageous levels. In finance, Black Monday refers to Monday, October 19, 1987, when stock markets around the world crashed, shedding a huge value in a very short time. The Dow Jones Industrial Average dropped by 508 points to 1738. During the decade of the 90s, however, millionaires multiplied by the thousands, and accounting irregularities were fairly rare or largely ignored.

Remember, these were the beginning days of MicroSoft. We hadn't even begun to envision a Google or Facebook, and Apple was just rolling out is first Mac products. Recruiting top talent and fighting off venture capitalists seemed the biggest problems that corporate executives faced. After surviving the Y2000 software scare and stumbling through a brief recession, we were rocked by September 11. The world changed. The principles espoused in our 1987 edition, however, didn't change – they became even more valid.

After a 15 year time span, in which we continued to explore the principles of ethical leadership and observe the practices of corporate leaders, I decided to write a second edition. So, in 2003, I revised the 1987 version not only with new insights based upon intimate involvement with hundreds of organizations, but also with concrete examples of the kind of corporate disasters that we predicted in 1987. Yes, we started the first few years of the new millennium with disgusting reports of corporate malfeasance by executives at Enron, Tyco, and Andersen consulting. And they only represented the tip of the iceberg. As it turned out, the first decade of the third century would usher in a financial crisis that nearly crippled the world economy and exposed the leaders of many of our banking and health care icons as fraudulent predators.

So, here we are, almost 30 years after the first edition. Corporate profits have never been higher. Income and opportunity inequality have never been greater. The Dow Jones has ridden the bull to over 18,000. And this lonely voice in the wilderness is making still one more plea to corporate leaders: Change your culture, elevate your consciousness – this is not sustainable!!

There are still two outstanding problems with the world economy: too much terror and too little trust. We can't do much about the first (including bombing ISIS and others to oblivion), but we can do a lot about the second. These two problems have made investments a treacherous proposition and management a perilous journey. Never before has it been so necessary for ethical leaders to navigate the economic sea and rebuild trust. We described the conditions in 1987 that were cause for concern and predicted the inevitable outcome of those conditions. In 2003, I described what happened with several corporations that engaged in unethical and fraudulent practices and predicted that worse would come if we didn't change. Since I am now in my 8th decade of life, and I don't want to write another plea when I'm 85, I will revisit the core principles of ethical leadership one last time with the hope that someone will hear the bell.

Its time to wake up and end the nightmares – to realize that ethical leadership is an essential part of the cure. We may need some legislative changes (e.g. carbon tax, higher mileage standards, less fracking that is more regulated, etc), but what we really need are dramatic changes in our culture and our consciousness that ethical leaders need to drive.

The purpose of this post is not to provide information to keep unethical executives out of jail, but to inspire leaders to elevate the level of their relationships with stakeholders and to think interdependently. Relationships are critical to the success of any organization. Those relationships include employees, shareholders, customers, and the communities in which they operate. For example, think manufacturing facilities in Sri Lanka and Bangaladesh.

Based on an extensive review of the literature on culture (See *Creating Organizational Soul*), and consciousness (See *The Consciousness Solution*), it appears that the required practices for ethical leadership and sustainable development are:

1. Challenge processes
2. Encourage the heart
3. Strive for congruence
4. Think long-term
5. Look at the whole
6. Tap employees' commitment, capability to learn, and desire to be helpful
7. Share power
8. Ensure diversity of voices

9. Create a humane and nurturing work environment
10. Build interdependent relationships
11. Foster community
12. Accept ownership and accountability
13. Resist policies of self-interest (e.g. executive compensation)
14. Put people and creativity at the center
15. Be authentic
16. Engage in constructive collaboration
17. Develop stories of integrity
18. Create a culture of trust

Why are these practices so difficult to institutionalize? The simple answer is that we are fighting history and habits. We live in a competitive culture that values independence and supports an economic system built on greed and self-interest. The best practices listed above require interdependent thinking and a focus on community. Leaders need to be more conscious about culture and more intentional about elevating consciousness. Unfortunately, leaders are still being rewarded for their behaviors. In the last several decades, the top 3% claimed all of the gains in wealth accumulation. The next 7% held even, and the lower 90% lost ground. Yes, the Dow Jones has gone from 1,700 to 18,000 since 1987. Corporate leaders managed to claim an inordinate amount of that 10x surge. The reward system is clearly reinforcing bad habits. Here are some key highs and lows of the Dow Jones over the past 30 years:

1982:   777
2,000: 11,700
2002:   7,200
2007:   14,000
2009:   6,500
2014:   17,000

It would be interesting to know who got hurt most by the lows and who benefitted the most from the highs. My bet is that the top 3% came out just fine and the lower 90% probably took the biggest hit. My prediction is that this bubble, like all others, will end. Irrational exuberance will quickly burst. The only way to avoid a long crash is to start thinking in terms of sustainable development, building ethical cultures and elevating consciousness.

Interdependence, culture, and consciousness bring us once again to the vital importance of relationships. Indeed, building interdependent relationships forms the core of ethical leadership.

In 1987, when we first published this book, essayist Myron Magnet observed that "as if trapped by a thermal inversion, the ethical atmosphere of business is growing acrid and the inhalation of those pernicious vapors could only lead to ever worse behaviors." While that observation was once a compelling metaphor, it is quickly becoming a terrifying reality. On September 21, 2014, I marched with 350,000 people who were trying to ring an alarm on Climate Change. Indeed, pernicious vapors are increasingly polluting our environment, threatening our water and food supply, melting our glaciers, killing species, and raising sea levels. While several corporations are finally stepping up and taking a leadership role, it still remains to be seen if leaders can make the large changes required in the small time frame available.

Leadership Lexicon

Leaders sometimes wonder why no one is following them. In most cases, the reason is because the leader does not possess all three essentials of effective leadership: Character, Commitment, and Competence. Leaders must be honest and ethical at their core, or people don't follow. Leaders must also be committed to developing themselves and others. If people are not convinced of the leader's commitment to their growth, they will not help the leader grow – and they will not follow. Finally, the leader needs to be seen as competent. But what does that mean?

In 2005, Bill O'Brien and I wrote the book *Leadership Lexicon*. The book emerged from work we were doing with the Merck Leadership Center. We were engaged to upgrade their leadership resource directory by identifying and describing observable behaviors that could be learned by Merck employees and be demonstrated through improved performance. Through that work we identified over 100 competencies that leaders may require to be effective in their jobs. Since it is virtually impossible to acquire and apply over 100 competencies, we organized all of them into the following 3x4 grid:

	Know and Grow Self	Know and Grow Your Team	Know and Grow Your Organization	Know and Grow Your Customers
Identify				
Build				
Drive				

As it turns out, all leadership competencies can be mapped into this model. While several boxes within the grid could contain multiple competencies, we have been able to identify the most critical competency for each box. Here is our vote for the 12 most important competencies of leadership:

	Know and Grow Self	Know and Grow Your Team	Know and Grow Your Organization	Know and Grow Your Customers
Identify	Strategic Thinking	Acquiring the Right Talent	Identifying Business Trends and Possibilities	Visioning and Positioning
Build	Personal Development	Building High Performing Teams	Building Organizational Capabilities	Building Partnerships
Drive	Problem Solving	Delegating	Aligning the Culture	Managing Complexity

Instead of diving into the myriad skills and behaviors that support all these leadership competencies, it's more important to understand leadership in its proper context. Here are some principles that may help with your own development as a leader.

1. <u>Leadership is not about charisma</u>. The real challenge for senior management is to create an environment where desired behaviors and results emerge naturally. Creating a collaborative culture is the enduring legacy of successful leaders.

2. <u>Leadership requires skills</u>. Take a guess. Which professionals spend the most, per capita, on golf lessons? Did you guess CEO's? How about marketing or sales VPs? The answer is professional golfers. The single biggest

differentiator in golf is golf skills. The same is true for leaders – not golf skills, but leadership skills. Skill development is different from knowledge acquisition. Knowledge gives us an understanding of the behavior. Skills give us the capability to perform new behaviors. I could read a thousand books on golf and still not be able to play well. If I take the time to learn and practice the skills, I may have a chance.

3. <u>Skills, once learned, require constant development and feedback</u>. Continuous improvement requires feedback. Another reason why experts in all fields continue to receive coaching and mentoring is because the feedback they receive on their performance increases their impact. Receiving accurate feedback will determine the rate and efficiency of your leadership development. Former New York City mayor Ed Koch was famous for asking "How am I doing?" This constant refrain helped to brand him as the "people's mayor."

4. <u>Leadership is not a place in an organization.</u> Most of us think of leadership as a noun. For example, we often talk about "the leadership" in our company. However, leadership is also a verb. Leadership is not a hierarchical place on an organizational chart. Rather, leadership is the response that every employee makes to the challenge or opportunity at hand at any given moment.

5. <u>Leaders stand out, for better or for worse.</u> Dr. William Anthony, a leader in the transformation of policy and clinical practice in the mental health field, once described leadership as follows: "When the battle begins and the shots ring out, everyone is targeting the leader." Leaders often create the conditions for change. As a result, others are asked to do

things differently. Leaders create new success criteria and change the rules of the game. By definition, then, leaders are often viewed as threats to the status quo and are often confronted by opposing forces. Anyone who tells you that he or she enjoyed the entire leadership experience has probably never experienced it in the first place.

Effective leaders are able to identify opportunities and threats, develop the programs and teams required to meet those challenges, and drive for results. Those are the meta-competencies of leadership: Identify, Build, and Drive. Leaders also need to know and grow themselves, their teams, their organizations, and their customers Having that "lexicon" at your fingertips, helps to navigate the vast and confusing literature on leadership development. Keep it simple. And lead.

Leadership Myths and Realities

Over 25 years ago, Barry Cohen and I published the book, *Leadership Myths and Realities*. Since that time we have held a variety of senior leadership positions and have continued to study the Art and Science of Leadership. This post will review the 10 myths and realities we wrote about in the late 80s, discuss their current relevance, and suggest any new myths and realities that have emerged. To be clear, myths usually contain some degree of truth. The point in this post is that, while the myth may be necessary, it is not necessarily sufficient – it's the expected table stakes. The reality suggests the additional possibilities that real leaders should take into account.

Myth: Leaders invest with financial capital. Reality: Leaders invest in human and information capital.

This myth and corresponding reality are more prevalent today than they were 25 years ago. Yes, we are seeing more and more mergers and acquisitions and corporate profits are soaring, but the real leaders and game-changers are those who invest in human capital and are constantly on top of new trends in science and technology. Human capital can be defined as those people who can respond rapidly to new changes and generate new sources of gain. After Robert Carkhuff introduced the terms in early 80s, the words human capital, information capital, and organizational capital have become common parlance. Most people refer to the time in which we are living as the Information Age. Carkhuff, our mentor for more than 40 years, suggests that

Richard Bellingham

we are really living in the Age of Ideation. Information that doesn't result in new ideas is not particularly helpful. Effective human processing is required to transform overwhelming information into useful ideas. Therefore, real leaders are not only adept at making sound financial investments, they also make wise investments in human, information, and organizational capital.

Myth: Leaders are risk takers. Reality: Leaders think creatively.

There has definitely been a shift in the last 25 years toward innovation and creativity. The difference between risk taking and creative thinking is that risk taking tends to be more like taking wild leaps into the unknown independent of the mission, whereas creative thinking means systematically processing multiple sources of information and generating ideas that advance the mission. Enron is a great example of risk taking that ended in disaster. The downfall of Enron was caused by highly intelligent people who were reinforced for taking enormous risks unrelated to the core business. More recently, the risk taking behind the financial crisis was fueled by dastardly manipulations of people (pushing mortgages on people who couldn't afford them) and products (derivatives, CDOs, junk bonds etc.). Even now, corporate and personal greed continue to push us into very vulnerable and risky territory. Real leaders take appropriate risks but also think creatively and take into account the potential implications of what they are doing. We are seeing more incubators being established to generate new ideas. We are seeing Universities, such as Cornell, starting Entrepreneurial Institutes. Almost all organizations are seeking ways to inculcate innovation in their cultures. And remember, in the last 25 years, we have seen the explosive growth of Apple, Google, and Facebook – all of which were based on creative thinking at its best. While Steve Jobs can be justly criticized for some of his leadership deficits, there is no question he was the epitome of creative thinking. His innovations transformed, and are continuing to transform, several industries.

Myth: Leaders manage my walking around. Reality: Leaders relate constructively.

While this myth and reality are as true today as they were 25 years ago, there have been some major variations on how they are played out. Now leaders are more likely to surf around a virtual environment instead of walking around the shop floor or visiting cubicles. Virtual visibility and accessibility have increased while physical presence has decreased. More importantly, the need to relate constructively has never been more necessary given the amount of time people spend gazing into their smart phones, tablets, or computer screens. The problem is that managers are still not particularly astute at picking up on non-verbal cues, listening attentively, and responding accurately to an employee's experience – it's ok to "walk around," but you have to know what to say when you engage staff in conversation. Constructive relationships are based on quality conversations that are team member focused and often team member led. The best selling Situational Leadership II Course developed by Pat Zigarmi at The Ken Blanchard Companies has established a dominant position in a huge market by teaching leaders how to relate more constructively with staff. This trend needs to continue.

Myth: Leaders manage change. Reality: Leaders initiate strategic changes.

While this myth and its corresponding reality have never been truer, there are still tons of money being pored into managing change vs. leading change. Managing change implies a reactive approach. Leaders are desperately trying to stay on top of all the changes with which they are constantly bombarded from disruptive technologies to climate change. It's essentially a hopeless case of Wack-A-Mole. Just as you think you've managed one change, another pops up. The reality is that leaders need to anticipate changes and stay ahead of the game. That means initiating strategic changes that are ahead of the curve. This is true in the geo-political arena as well. If world leaders try to manage all the changes that are taking place in the Middle East, it is a hopeless cause. They need to work together to initiate strategic changes that give peace and prosperity a chance.

Myth: Leaders develop people through training. Reality: Leaders create an environment that nurtures personal development.

Organizations still spend billions of dollars training their people. Unfortunately, most of the training is incomplete, over-lapping, or redundant. As an example, one of the largest banks in the world just invested millions of dollars training people in how to create a trustworthy organization. They put all mid-level managers through intensive training in an attempt to change the negative perceptions that the public held toward its banking practices. Strange as it may seem, this same bank continued to engage in unethical and misleading practices, not seeming to appreciate the impact of leaders telling employees to do one thing and then doing completely the opposite themselves. Real change comes when a serious effort is made to align the culture with the strategy and to create a healthy, innovative, ethical, and productive work environment. In the last 25 years, I have seen many companies spend a lot of time, energy, and resources trying to change their cultures. What I haven't seen is a willingness to measure that change and to form a "soul committee" whose sole responsibility is to point out the gaps between stated goals and day-to-day behaviors. Unless leaders are willing to embrace "court jesters" they will continue to pour dollars down the sinkhole by assuming a training program will achieve it's intended results without paying attention to the culture.

Myth: Leaders emphasize product quality. Leaders emphasize product, process, people, and customer benefits.

There is no question that product quality is still required to be successful in this competitive global environment. Apple's amazing success story is built on excellent products. American automobile companies can't compete with cars that don't match the quality of cars in Europe and Asia. Pharmaceutical companies depend on the public perception that their products are safe and of the highest quality. J&J actually turned the Tylenol disaster into a public relations victory by showing the world how committed it was to providing quality products. But, especially now, quality products are not enough. There has to be an equal focus on process, people, technology, culture, and customer benefits. The success of Lean Start-Ups depends on early customer verification of the benefits a new product provides. As the need for continuous generation of new ideas increases, people and process assume more and more importance.

Myth: Leaders motivate employees. Reality: Leaders free exemplars.

Not much has changed in the last 25 years on this myth and reality pair. Leaders still don't tailor rewards according to the level of functioning of their employees and people who are outside the normal curve are more likely to be punished than freed. Let's start with the first problem. Motivational strategies need to be tailored to the level of functioning of the person you want to motivate. Leaders usually try to motivate detractors with carrots and sticks. They attempt to motivate observers with tangible rewards, i.e. if you do "x", I will give you "y." Participants (solid performers who meet expectations) are usually recognized for excellent performance. Leaders usually try to motivate contributors with more responsibility and accountability. And leaders attempt to motivate leaders by freeing them to initiate. The second problem (punishing exemplars) also still exists. When someone is performing 3 standard deviations from the mean, they are more likely to be punished than rewarded. I have plenty of evidence to support this claim. I was once asked to review all of the leadership development programs of one of the leading pharmaceutical companies in the world. In one class, the instructor showed a video of a team on which one person was clearly the most intelligent and most productive member. Instead of freeing that person to generate new possibilities that would help the company, they punished him for not being a "team player." The video was intended to convey the point that conforming to the norm was more important than initiating new ideas. The reality is that leaders can't motivate employees; they can only align rewards with their level of functioning. Leaders can inspire employees as role models and by articulating an aspirational vision, but they can't motivate them with empty motivational speeches, blanket programs, or by insisting they conform to the norm. The reality is that leaders can create optimally motivating environments by framing the work people are doing as purposeful and meaningful, by fostering collaboration, by adding variety, by supporting growth, and by providing opportunities for development. Then, people will choose to be optimally motivated.

Myth: Leaders always seek consensus. Reality: Leaders make fine discriminations on how to lead.

Leaders still tend to be "one-shot cowboys." They latch onto a leadership style that fits their comfort zone and then stay with that style independent of staff reactions. The best leaders not only make effective choices about when to be authoritative, persuasive, participative, consultative, or empowering, they also have a large repertoire of responses for each of those styles. Fine discriminations are based on accurate assessments of the commitment, capability, and cultural background of the person with whom they are dealing. The pendulum is always swinging back and forth from more supportive to more directive. One is as likely to fail as the other without an accurate discrimination of the situational requirements as well as the motivation and skill of the person it is supposed to effect. Situational Leadership II has made a significant contribution to addressing this myth and creating a new reality, but there is still a long way to go. The reality is that command and control leadership can be the most effective style in certain situations, particularly when a leader is setting strategy or there is a need to teach someone a skill as quickly as possible.

Myth: Leaders manage time. Reality: Leaders do the right things right.

We continue to hear a great deal about time management and new approaches for making the best use of your time. Simple approaches like writing down priorities for the day and then reflecting for a few minutes each hour on how well you are focusing on those priorities have helped leaders make sure they are spending their time on the right tasks. An obsession with efficiency, however, can get in the way of what's most effective. With conditions changing as rapidly as they are, great leaders need to process information constantly and decide what requires their focus. Can you imagine being the President of the United States and trying to decide where to invest your time. Should you focus on ensuring that people have health care, containing an Ebola crisis in Africa, dealing with a terrorist threat in Syria, finding a two state solution for Israel, improving our educational system, restoring our infrastructure, responding to a natural disaster (e.g. fires, hurricanes, etc.) or attending to a racial issue in Ferguson, Missouri. It's endless. And leaders of most organizations face long lists of daunting challenges each day as well. While it is true that effective leaders need to manage their time, the reality is that they need to make conscious choices about investing their precious time where it will have the most impact. This myth-reality pair has only become more imperative in the last 25 years as leaders are expected to do more with less.

Myth: Leaders support individual wellness programs.
Reality: Leaders develop healthy organizational cultures.

This list of myths and realities would not be complete without addressing the issue of wellness. 25 years ago, we developed the most comprehensive, culture-based program in the country. At the time, national health care costs were still far short of one trillion dollars per year. Now they are approaching three trillion dollars. Corporations are paying a large share of those costs. At AT&T, we not only demonstrated cost savings of over 300 million dollars over a 10 year period based on reduction of risks between a control group and an experimental group, we also demonstrated significant gains in job satisfaction and productivity. Even with those results and with rapidly escalating health care costs, corporate leaders have not adopted comprehensive, culture-based solutions for creating a healthier, more productive workforce. When I say culture based, I mean auditing the norms and values of the workplace as well as blood pressure and cholesterol levels of the workers. At AT&T, we initiated the Total Life Concept (TLC) program with a Managing for Health and Productivity seminar that helped leaders understand how their behaviors contributed to either high-level wellness or low-level worseness. After 25 years, organizations are still stuck in the rut of fitness and stress programs without addressing the cause of sedentary living and excessive stress – dysfunctional leadership behaviors.

So it appears that the 10 leadership myths and realities we proposed 25 years ago still have relevance today. Based on our experience and changing economic conditions, we would now add a few more myths and realities to the list:

Myth: Leaders stay focused on how to get things done. Reality: Leaders keep everyone focused on why the work needs to be done.

Yes, leaders are expected to get results. They need to be clear about what needs to get done and must possess a good sense of how to get it done. More importantly, however, is the need to stick with the principle of purpose before action – to encourage people to ask "why?" before they rush to judgment and create detailed action plans. Why will consumers love this product or service? Why do people need a smart watch? Why is solution A better than solution B? Why do we believe we will have a different outcome in Syria than we had in Iraq or Afghanistan – or Vietnam for that matter? Taking the time to reflect on an action before jumping in may be one of the strongest requirements for leaders. Leaders need to be resourceful, respectful, and restrained. Exercising restraint in the face of pressure means taking the time to live in the right question instead of jumping into the wrong action. The best leaders are decisive AND accurate. Being accurate demands taking time to reflect and ask why.

Myth: Leadership is a function of one person. Leadership is a team of committed and complementary people.

While there are times when one person needs to step up and take charge, the most profound changes occur when everyone assumes leadership for accomplishing the mission. Clearly, the world can be thankful that Churchill assumed command of the situation in Europe and refused to negotiate with Hitler and the Nazis in World War II. In most cases, however, servant leadership produces greater results than hero leadership. In the book, *Spiritual Leadership*, I differentiate between sole leadership vs. soul leadership. Developing a diverse group of highly committed people who can create an organizational soul is preferential to one person flying solo and going it alone on all matters.

Myth: Leaders create followers. Reality: Leaders create leaders.

Charismatic leaders who stir up the passion of their followers may yield short-term results, but most gurus end up being corrupted. Their egos usually lead them to make self-indulgent decisions and to give in to narcissistic behaviors. Real leaders inspire people to mobilize behind a cause, but devote most of their energy to developing leaders who can sustain and elevate the mission over the long term. Followers tend to become dependent on the leader and competitive with each other for the leader's favor. In the worst cases, the exchange is favors for favor. People who grow into leadership roles tend to be more concerned with making a contribution and making a difference than stroking the leader's ego.

Myth: Leaders help people get what they want. Reality: Leaders help people do what they need.

Good leaders usually are tuned into the dreams and aspirations of people who work with them. And they look for opportunities for them to develop the skills they need to accomplish what they want. Great leaders inspire others to raise the bar and accomplish more than what they may have thought was possible. If you believe that the purpose of life is grow, then leaders help people do what they need to do to grow – even if there is initial resistance and doubt. Great leaders help people align behind a mission that is greater than themselves, whether the mission relates to the team, the organization, the community, or the world. So, the ten myths and realities we identified 25 years ago are still relevant today. Changing conditions and deeper experience led us to add a few more to the list.

RI3C7K's Profiles in Leadership

There is no such thing as a generic profile for leaders. The right blend of skills, experience, knowledge, characteristics, and attitude depends on the requirements of the situation in which the leader finds herself. This post will look at several leaders who were successful in a variety of fields with totally different conditions and contexts. There are two common themes among all of these leaders - they all had enormous impact and they all exhibited multiple degrees of RI3C7K's profile – you'll need to read to the end to find out what that means.

Jesus is a good place to start this journey. According to the best historical sources, Jesus was an illiterate Jew who was born and raised in Nazareth as a carpenter's son. As a result of his enormous charisma, he was able to mobilize a band of Jews to protest the oppression of the Roman authorities. He was found guilty of sedition and crucified along with several thousand other Jews. Between the years 70 and 120 CE, several people who were influenced by his teaching of love and service and his commitment to justice and fairness wrote gospels or letters to explain/interpret his life. In order to avoid the on-going wrath of the Romans, four of the "writers" – not written by one hand and certainly not the earliest followers - published Matthew, Mark, Luke, and John, distanced themselves from the Jews (all of the disciples of Jesus), and were selected among the manuscripts of the time by Constantine during the 4th Century to be included in the New Testament. During this complex and multi-faceted time, the creation, incubation, and activation of

Christianity began. Independent of your reactions to this simplified version of history, the question remains, "What were the leadership characteristics of Jesus that resulted in the centuries of influence he has had?" For me, Jesus was a great leader because he demonstrated the fullest possible commitment, he was an incredibly capable preacher and teacher, he understood the culture in which he was living, he responded to the deepest values of his followers, he showed the true meaning of compassion through his words and behaviors, and he demonstrated amazing courage by challenging authority, cultural norms, and religious certainty, i.e. telling truth to power. He knew what was profoundly important and acted on it, even when his actions cost him his life. No other leader since has even approached what he accomplished – two billion followers 2,000 years after his death. A list of terrific books on the historical Jesus are at the end of this post.

Jumping ahead to more recent times, Churchill is the political leader who had the most impact in the last century. We owe our escape from Nazi tyranny to his unflappable courage and resolve during WWII. Unlike Jesus, Churchill was born into an aristocratic family. He started life with disadvantages he never wholly conquered, although his whole career was an effort to overcome them. Only a man who knew and faced despair within himself could carry conviction at such a moment. Only a man who knew what it was to discern a gleam of hope in a hopeless situation, whose courage was beyond reason, and whose aggressive spirit burned at its fiercest when he was surrounded by enemies could give emotional reality to the words of defiance which rallied and sustained all who heard him in the menacing summer of 1940. Churchill suffered from prolonged and recurrent fits of depression; and no understanding of his character is possible unless this central fact is taken into account. A depressed person forces himself into activity, and denies himself rest or relaxation because he cannot afford to stop. Churchill relied on creative energy as an effective defense against depression. In addition to being depressed, Churchill also felt cheated by his physique. He was small in stature with thin, un-muscular limbs, and delicate hands; and he spoke with a lisp and a slight stutter. He only grew to 5 feet, six inches. As a consequence of his "unmanly appearance," he was beaten and bullied at school. The courage he consistently, and sometimes rashly, displayed was not based upon any natural superiority of physique, but rather upon his determination to be tough in spite of his lack of height and muscle. This toughness sometimes spilled over into aggressiveness and dominance that are not normally words that describe great leaders but were required to face Hitler's killing machine. In addition to being depressed emotionally and small physically, Churchill was born prematurely and received remarkably little affection or support from either parent in the vital years of early childhood. Perhaps the most obvious trait he developed as a response to his deprivation was ambition – a powerful force he was powerless to resist. So, again, the question becomes, "What were the leadership characteristics of Churchill that resulted in the profound, unwavering leadership during his time?" Like Jesus, Churchill demonstrated incredible conviction and commitment, he possessed the courage to stand up to a tyrant and to a country in favor of appeasement, and he was responsive to the deepest values and strongest feelings of his fellow citizens. He didn't demonstrate much compassion or sensitivity to others, but he used his creative energy to overcome daunting odds.

Stepping back to the previous century, Kafka was a literary leader who was not only a great scholar, but also was scrupulously honest. With strangers, Kafka was always ill at ease. In 1913, he writes, "If I am in an unfamiliar place, among a number of strange people, or people whom I feel to be strangers, then the whole room presses on my chest and I am unable to move, my whole personality seems virtually to get under their skins, and everything becomes hopeless." Like Churchill, Kafka regarded his own body with distaste and compared it unfavorably with that of his father. He writes, "I remember how we often undressed together in the same bathing-hut. There I was: skinny, weakly, slight whereas my father was strong, tall, and broad. Even inside the hut I felt myself a miserable specimen, and what's more, not only in my father's eyes, but in the eyes of the whole world, for he was for me the measure of all things." Perhaps as a result of his physical and emotional suffering as a child, Kafka was unequaled in his ability to articulate fears that lurk in the recesses of the mind. Clearly, his two most famous literary achievements, *The Trial* and *Metamorphosis*, are testaments to that ability. So why is Kafka included in profiles in leadership? For me, Kafka was totally self-aware and had the courage to express himself in unique and creative ways. Again, when talking about leaders, it's essential to start with the requirements they face, not simply look at generic and traditional characteristics like being male 6 feet 2, muscular, and emotionally stable. Kafka had the courage to look deeply inside and to share his insights with the world – those are the requirements for literary leadership.

Staying with the turn of the century, and turning to the power of female leadership, Jane Addams was a social reformer and peace activist, led the American settlement house movement, and founded its most famous settlement, Chicago's Hull House (1889). Addams was born in Cedarville, Illinois in 1860 and graduated from Rockville College in 1882. In 1889, she founded Chicago's Hull House, where she lived and worked until her death in 1935. A home and gathering place for reformers who "settled" in the neighborhoods they served, settlements brought a broad range of social services to immigrants and the urban poor. Believing settlements were a space where all classes could meet to solve problems of urban industrialization, Addams assembled a cohort of brilliant women around her whose innovative solutions shaped 20th century social policy. Responding to community needs, the women of Hull House pioneered in bringing social services to immigrant and working class neighborhoods. They set up day care for children, founded playgrounds, delivered health services, and studied toxic substances in factories. They investigated slums (founding the profession of urban sociology), brought about passage of factory inspections, pushed for ending child labor, improved tenement conditions and sweatshops, fought for shorter hours, higher wages, protective labor laws, and established the nation's first juvenile court. An outspoken supporter of labor, Addams was also a gifted lecturer and prolific writer. Her most famous book was <u>Twenty Years at Hull House</u>(1910). A staunch suffrage supporter, she was Vice President of the NAWSA, and wrote and spoke widely about the vote's importance to women. She founded and chaired the Woman's Peace Party (1915), was first president of the Women's International League for Peace and Freedom (1919), and was awarded the Nobel Peace Prize (1931) for her years of peace activism. The abridgment of civil liberties and attacks on pacifists in World War I (she was vilified as a traitor for opposing the war), led Addams to help found the American Civil Liberties Union (1920). She died at 74, her work for social justice having impacted every aspect of American life. For inclusion in RICK's profiles in leadership, Jane stood out for her courage, compassion, collaboration, initiative, and integrity.

From these largely divergent examples of spiritual leadership, political leadership, literary leadership, and social leadership we can derive some critical characteristics of leaders. The desired combination of these characteristics varies depending upon the requirements of the situation. I've captured those characteristics with the acronym RI^3C^7K in which

$R =$ Responsiveness
$I^3 =$
- Initiative
- Interdependence
- Integrity

$C^7 =$
- Commitment
- Capability
- Cultural Sensitivity
- Compassion
- Collaboration
- Courage
- Creativity

$K =$ Kick-Ass Knowledge

There is no generic set of characteristics for a leader. Leaders don't always fall into our conventional views about what leaders look like, how they act, or what their family history is. And picking great leaders always means identifying the requirements first.

Source Books for this post:

Christ Actually, James Carroll
Zealot, Reza Aslan
The Gnostic Gospels, Elaine Pagels
The Case for God, Karen Armstrong
The Evolution of God, Robert Wright
Good without God, Greg Epstein
Indispensible: When Leaders Really Matter, Gautam Mukunda
Churchill's Black Dog, Kafka's Mice, Anthony Storr
Profiles in Leadership, Walter Isaacson

Social Health

Just as strong leadership is a requirement for creating a healthy organization, sound education is the fundamental requirement for a healthy society. The lead article addresses all the factors that need to be taken into account with educational reform.

The second post, History of Great Ideas, explains why big ideas never seem to take hold. Jesus laid out in elaborate detail how we should live our lives, but we still break the key principles with reckless abandon, e.g. love your neighbor as you love yourself, turn the other cheek, etc.

The third post, Inequality, deals with the outcome of educational disparity as well as the diminishments of game-changing ideas. When we abandon the guiding principles for leading responsible lives, we end up with huge gaps between the "haves" and the "have nots."

The fourth post, Interdependence, addresses the attitude and orientation required to create a more equitable and just society. To the extent that we continue to just look out for ourselves, we create the conditions for more revolution and revolt.

The fifth post, Symptoms and Systems, reveals the basic fault that society commits when it reacts to symptoms instead of taking proactive approaches to changing the systems creating the problems. It represents a shift from treatment to prevention.

The sixth post, Harmonious Inclusion, explains the differential results of exclusivity vs. inclusivity and the potential of tapping into each person's unique gifts. It suggests that our goal should be to look for ways of bringing out the best in people instead of discarding them in societies' garbage bins.

The seventh post, Abuse, expands the meaning of neglect and deals with the sins of omission as well as commission. It is a compelling case for caring more carefully for all species in our environment.

This chapter argues that a healthy society requires greater attention to education, inequality, interdependence, inclusivity, systemic change, and caring concern.

Integrated Educational Reform

If there were ever an area in need of exceptional leadership, it's educational reform. The book, *Teacher Wars,* by Dana Goldstein, presents the most comprehensive review of educational reform efforts I have seen in the 40 years I have been reading on the subject. It provides solid, research-based insights on what works and what doesn't work in education. The book points out that accountability and value added measurement are the current rage and are the major influencers in educational policy from "No Child Left Behind" to "Race to the Top." My concern over a long history of educational involvement at multiple levels (elementary education, inmate rehabilitation, adult learning, wellness programming, leadership development, and university teaching) is that we tend to pick an issue of the day (e.g. accountability) and fail to take into account all the required factors for effective educational reform. True reform requires strong leadership and change management. In my view, the five broad categories are components, functions, processes, conditions, and standards. All of these factors need to be seen as critical elements of an integrated system. Let's take a look at each one.

Components. Traditionally, discussions about the right components revolved around reading, writing, math, and science. A focus on the right components usually results in content wars, e.g. what is the best reading program?, what is the best way to teach math?, where do the arts and PE fit in the mix? A mentor of mine, Robert Carkhuff, has proposed the most radical reform idea I have seen in the content arena.

He suggests that we adopt a new 3Rs of education: Relate, Reason, and Represent. Our ability to *relate* to information is directly dependent on our reading, writing, and math skills, so this reform proposal does not throw the baby out with the bath. It simply puts it into a larger context and gives the learner a good reason to learn the basic navigational tools of learning. The idea also encourages the learner to *relate* constructively to people as well as to information – a rather key component of our ability to serve as productive citizens. Our ability to *reason* depends on our capability for comprehension and our ability to think. Our ability to *represent* depends on our writing skills as well as our ability to think multi-dimensionally. As I mentioned earlier, our deficiency in this area has led to hundreds of failed reform efforts that relied on a single factor instead of *representing* the solution as a multi-faceted, interconnected system of all success factors. I happen to think that the New 3Rs makes good sense, but the point is that educational components only comprise one part of the equation. We need to step out of the quagmire of content wars and see the larger picture.

Functions: As I see it, the three main functions of education are to learn, to think, and to create. We need to learn how to learn, learn critical content, and learn how to access the rapidly exploding body of information that is available to us. Memorizing facts to pass tests is no longer sufficient to compete in a global environment. With information doubling at shorter and shorter time intervals, it is increasingly important to be able to process all the information and think about implications and possibilities in entirely new ways. Also, as the rapid advances in innovation have demonstrated, we can no longer depend on a certain set of skills and knowledge maintaining their relevance over time. We need to constantly generate new ideas and develop new skills that enable us to differentiate ourselves in a competitive environment. Clearly, there are other functions of education beyond learning, thinking, and creating, but these seem most important to me.

Processes: In *Teacher Wars*, Goldstein summarizes a vast body of research that highlights what seems to be most effective in the teaching process. Three key variables emerged: Set high expectations, regularly assess starting points and progress, and personalize learning goals and methods for each learner. Part of setting high expectations is that you have to believe that every learner can learn even though the pace may be different. If you don't believe children can learn, they probably won't. Being able to personalize learning means developing individual educational plans for each learner. It is also means being able to relate to each kid's feelings, experience, and learning style. David Aspy once summarized all of educational research as "kids learn from people they like." If you can't respond to a kids' experience and personalize their leaning, it is unlikely they will like you. And it is unlikely they will learn.

Conditions: It has become increasingly clear that teacher effectiveness is only one factor that accounts for kids' ability to learn and develop. The student's home environment, the school environment, and the overall community environment all play roles. Kids from low income, single parent homes are less likely to succeed as kids who come from affluent, privileged backgrounds. If children are more worried about getting home safely due to gangs and drugs than they are concerned about completing their homework, then their chances of success are diminished. Recent research demonstrates clearly that academic performance is directly related to the number of words that kids hear in the first 4 years of their life. If they enter school having grown up in an abusive environment and having listened to very few books, the chances for success are slim. Conditions also apply to teachers. If teachers feel like they are constantly demonized, scrutinized, and marginalized, they are unlikely to feel very buoyant about their career. Similarly, if a school is under-staffed, under-resourced, and under-valued, then the culture of the school is less likely to be stimulating and supportive. The point is that learning conditions and cultures have to be taken fully into account for educational reform to be effective and sustainable.

Standards: And now we come to the factor that is currently getting the most attention. There are wide ranging and deep debates about how teachers are evaluated and how much weight student performance gets in the formula. Value added measurement looks at how much progress individual students have made between two points in time. Complex formulas are being developed to predict what a reasonable expectation should be (e.g. two reading levels in one year) given the composition of the class and other factors that could affect learning. The goal is to measure how much value the teacher adds taking into account all other variables. Clearly, this is a difficult bar to achieve. In addition to trying to reach agreement on what gets measured, how each factor is weighed, and who performs the measurement, this process is also held hostage by the amount of time and money it takes to conduct the evaluation. The goal of any research is to control for as many variables as possible and isolate the key factors that actually make a difference or not. For me, standards for school performance, teacher performance, and school performance are all vital. They need to be as simple and fair as possible and be administered in a way that doesn't require excessive time, training, and money. Having created some of the most comprehensive performance evaluation systems for the most prestigious companies in the world, I have waded through the deep puddles of this problem. I can say with a lot of dirt on my feet, that it is hard to find a way to come out clean.

But to come back to the overall goal of this post, my belief is that all five factors need to be addressed and we need to see the inter-relationship among all of them. And it takes extraordinary leadership at all levels to get constituents to focus on more than one variable at a time. It's inappropriate to place all the blame on teachers or students when many factors come into play. It's also inappropriate to place all your hope on a single intervention when the entire system requires transformation.

In my work building healthy, innovative, and productive work environments, I have found Patrick Lencioni's work on dysfunctional organizations to be very helpful and relevant to this issue. Lencioni suggests there are four building blocks to achieving great results: Trust, Healthy Conflict, Commitment, and Accountability. In his experience, you can't achieve great results by focusing solely on accountability. It is also necessary to build trust, engage in healthy conflict, and develop commitment to the goals and plans. In the current educational reform environment, there is very little trust and lots of unhealthy conflict - whether it's the union stance around tenure or the best literacy program for each type of student. If educational reform is going to be successful, we need to start with trust and healthy conflict. Those two building blocks are dependent on great leadership.

In my view, commitment is not the major issue. Having been married to an extraordinary special education teacher and having raised a daughter who is now teaching at Columbia Teachers College, I don't see a lack of teacher commitment as the biggest problem. To me, capability and culture are far more potent variables in the success equation. Teachers are currently receiving minimal amounts of professional development and most are not prepared to deal with all the classroom management, lesson planning, teaching delivery, and administrative requirements they must face on a daily basis – not to mention a classroom of technology-savvy, entertainment- addicted, demographically and learning-diverse students.

The title of this post, integrated educational reform, was intended to suggest that all factors need to be taken into account if we are going to achieve effective and sustainable change. And that accounting can only take place under the vision of extraordinary leaders at all levels. The title also alludes to another major challenge underlying the whole reform movement. After the Civil Rights Act of 1964, the primary focus was on integration, not accountability. The pendulum has now swung to the other side, at the expense of more serious efforts to integrate racially and economically. Our schools have become more segregated in the last 30 years, and our student populations are suffering the consequences of the severe income inequality gap that has insidiously poisoned our culture and our economy. Americans live, learn, and work in more unequal ways than they ever have in the past. So integrated educational reform means changing our systems as well as our shared values. It can be done, but it won't be easy and there are no "one factor solutions" that can possibly pull it off . . . . . . and pull us up on the list of countries with the best educational systems.

History of Great Ideas

Great ideas have piling up in history's graveyard for 3,000 years. They are left unattended and largely forgotten. These ideas are usually met with laudatory excitement and abundant enthusiasm when they are first introduced. Then, the ideas are gradually diminished and distorted through this four step process:

- Trivialization
- Bastardization
- Privatization
- Commercialization

Trivialization occurs when the idea is too large for people to comprehend and embrace. In order to make the idea more understandable, it is made smaller, dumbed down, or reduced to a more palatable size.

Bastardization occurs when the idea, already reduced, becomes convoluted by misunderstanding and distortion. In order to make the idea consistent with any given set of biases, inferences, assumptions, or beliefs, the idea gets twisted to support a preferred ideology.

Privatization occurs when someone claims the idea as an original innovation. In order to feed their imagination of creativity and superiority, opportunists take credit for the ideas, already in their reduced form, that rightfully belong to others.

Commercialization occurs when the false owner figures out how to capitalize on the idea and make money. At this point, the idea is packaged, marketed, and sold to satisfy whatever material desires the idea thief has independent of the idea's initial intent and value.

Two ideas, among thousands, that have been victimized by this historical process are Wellness and Human Capital Development. I will take you through the process below.

Wellness: This great idea started out with the intention of helping people become more balanced, unified, and conscious. It began as an integrated approach to improve health physically, emotionally, intellectually, and spiritually. It proposed a wholistic methodology to health that maximized energy using a play on Einstein's formula: $E = MC^2$ (Energy = Motivation times Competency Squared). In its comprehensive form, wellness included risk reduction and performance enhancement. The mission of organizational wellness programs was to create an environment that supports positive health practice. The environmental component addressed the norms and values of the workplace as well as management behaviors.

This idea was quickly trivialized by reducing it to its least potent component: physical health. It became bastardized when charlatans started making false claims about the health benefits of certain vitamin supplements or by guarantees of extended longevity through one practice or another. The idea was rapidly privatized when individuals boasted of new breakthroughs in health and fitness. Finally, companies jumped on the bandwagon and started selling wellness programs that had little or no connection to the original idea.

Human Capital Development: This great idea, originated by Dr. Robert Carkhuff in the early 80s, was initially intended to bolster economic productivity growth by continually generating new sources of gain through mulit-dimensional thinking and organizational processing. It began as an attempt to create an interdependent eco-system of schools, businesses, government agencies, and homes that would elevate the performance and productivity of people around the world.

The idea was quickly trivialized by making it a sub-set of HR departments and by equating it with training and development. It was bastardized by associating the name with personnel administration. Many consulting firms quickly adopted the name and created billion dollar businesses under the umbrella of Human Capital, thus completing the last two steps of the historically engrained process.

Many organizations now discharge the responsibility for Human Capital development to their HR departments. Talent Management divisions of HR create vision statements proclaiming to develop and free human capital. Very few of the activities stay connected to the original idea of enabling people to think multi-dimensionally, generate new ideas, and create interdependent networks. Even Talent Management with its components of attracting, selecting, assessing, developing, deploying, rewarding, and retaining highly valued employees approaches the process in fragmented and sub-optimal ways. There are still very few integrated and optimized talent management systems in organizations today.

I could go through many more examples, but I'm not interested in visiting the graveyard of great ideas that have been reduced to trivialized commercialization. I'm interested not only in re-connecting to great ideas as they were originally conceptualized, but also to protect new ideas that are still in their fragile beginnings. By increasing awareness of this process, I would like to bring back to life some of the best ideas and nurture new ideas. We know that game-changing ideas usually come from the margins whether they are new technologies conceived in a garage or new ideas generated in think tanks. These new ideas creatively destroy the way we perceive the world, see ourselves and envision our own possibilities.

In organizations, this same process applies. Ideas created at the margins are vulnerable to the pull of "normalization" and are then drawn under the bell curve. Innovation in organizations faces an uphill battle because of the staid cultures in which they are born. Cultural immune systems are very good at organ rejection, i.e. killing any idea that threatens the "way things work around here." That's why many organizations have established skunk works and incubators that enable ideas to grow without the threats of trivialization and bastardization. As Nietzsche said, "It is only the great thought that gives greatness to an action."

The good news is that there are ideas emerging right now that could totally change the kind of lives we live and the kind of world we live in. Dr. Artie Egendorf, a Harvard educated, Vietnam Veteran polymath has founded Energy's

Way to enable us to supercharge our very being. Due Quach, a Harvard/Wharton educated, Vietnam boat survivor, has developed a methodology for helping inner city kids build resiliency and Calm Clarity – the name of her new institute. Luke Chan, a qigong master in China is translating the Tao te Ching (The Way of Life) that was originally written 2,600 years ago by Lao Tsu. He is trying to breathe new life into one of greatest sets of ideas ever written. These are all ideas that could make a profound difference in the world if we can protect them from the historical process that typically diminishes or kills them.

Inequality

Imagine a picture of the downtown area of NYC – home of Wall Street. It's a beautiful sight with majestic buildings, but there is a story unfolding that is as ugly as the buildings are beautiful. In those spectacular buildings, and in others around the world, evil lurks. Here are some facts.

The highest percentage of ultra high net worth people (greater than $30 million) lives in NYC. Unfortunately, almost 50% of the people who live in NYC earn less than 1.5 of poverty income. That is a gaping juxtaposition of ultra wealthy and ultra poor. In fact, in the US, inequality is back to where it was before the Great Depression. The richest 1 per cent captured 95 per cent of all income gains since 2009, while the bottom 90 per cent got poorer

America is not alone, however, in the universe of inequality. The net worth of India's billionaire community has soared 12-fold in 15 years - enough to eliminate absolute poverty twice over in the country, where income inequality is also on the rise.

Seven out of ten people in the world today live in countries where inequality has increased over the past three decades. Shockingly, the richest 85 people in the world own the same amount of wealth as the bottom half of the world's population

In Thomas Piketty's book, *Capital,* he exposes the wide inequality gaps in income and wealth that have emerged over the past 300 years. Piketty suggests that previous economic analysis had neither the access to information nor the power of statistical tools that we have today. His current analysis is scary and depressing.

Piketty poses the question, are wealth and income inequalities convergent or divergent trends, i.e. will the gap grow in the next century or will the gap diminish? His research, based on 2,000 years of historical data across the globe, indicates that the gap is more like to widen than narrow.

His analysis reveals that in the US, 5% claim over 30% of the income and almost 70% of the wealth in the country. With decreasing growth rates across the world and increased capital in the hands of the wealthy, there is reason to believe that the disparity could become even more absurd. The gap has almost doubled in the last 30 years and there is no counter-balancing force that could reverse the trend.

Sadly, the game is rigged from the start. If you start out rich, you have a much better chance of staying rich than someone who comes from poverty. In their 2005 paper "The Opportunity Cost of Admission Preferences at Elite Universities," Princeton scholars Thomas Espenshade and Chang Chung found that legacy status gives fortunate applicants the equivalent of an additional 160 points on the former 1,600 point SAT scale. One hundred sixty points is no small adjustment; on the contrary, it's the sort of improvement hopeful high school students bury their noses in books for. Yet it comes gratis to a set of students already privileged enough to be born to graduates of prestigious institutions. And, to add fuel to the fire, the privileged students are more likely to get the tutoring and resume building experiences than their less fortunate competitors for those treasured slots in the best universities.

Legacy preference seems to intensify in effect toward the upper end of university rankings, rendering entry into prestigious institutions with valuable resources and facilities especially daunting for poor students without alumni parents. Journalist Daniel Golden reports that nearly 90 percent of elite institutions calibrate their scales in favor of legacy status when weighing applicants against one another; as a result, numerous top-tier universities feature legacy acceptance rates far higher than overall acceptance rates. Legacy, in other words, is a sort of affirmative action for the wealthy.

And what is our response to this unfair playing field? Gut Affirmative Action for the poor and disenfranchised. Between 1996 and 1998 California and Texas eliminated the use of affirmative action in college and university admissions. At the states' elite public universities admission rates of black and Hispanic students fell by 30-50 percent and minority representation in the entering freshman classes declined. The inequality problem is clearly trending in the wrong direction.

Through some combination of all those factors arises a path to power: Research by Thomas Dye of the Lincoln Center for Public Service shows that 54 percent of America's corporate leaders as well as 42 percent of our government officials are all graduates of just 12 institutions – Yale, Harvard, Princeton and Stanford among them. In 2003, Harvard accepted 40 percent of legacy applicants compared to an overall 11 percent acceptance rate; Princeton's numbers are quite similar. As a result, there are 25 rich kids for every poor kid in the elite universities.

It appears there are powerful forces working against any efforts to even the playing field or reduce inequality. People in power want to stay in power and they will do whatever they can to hold onto their cherished position. The three strategies are:

1. Consolidate power
2. Eliminate diversity
3. Impose "truth"

As long as the people with money and influence continue to pursue those strategies, there is not much hope for closing the gaps. In my mind, the only solution is a change in consciousness. Inequality is caused by people with competitive and acquiring minds vs. compassionate and inquiring minds.

Interdependence

Imagine a struggling polar bear in the Arctic Circle. This bear is at risk of extinction because we have failed to recognize that we are a part of an interdependent ecosystem. As a result of human behavior, the climate is changing so rapidly that the ice melt is threatening the bear's ability to find food. This may be the fate of humans if we don't elevate our consciousness.

In a recent article in the New York Times, Roger Cohen wrote eloquently about the need for interdependence. He reported on a conference on "Inclusive Capitalism" at which Mark Carney, the Canadian governor of the Bank of England suggested that the core problem of the financial crisis has not gone away. Cohen summarized, "the deep unease and anger in developed countries about the ways globalization and technology magnify returns for the super-rich, operating in a world of low taxation and lax regulation where short-term gain becomes a guiding principle, even as societies become more unequal, offering diminished opportunities to the young, less community, and a growing sense of unfairness. As Bill Clinton noted a couple of hours before Carney's speech, the first reaction of human beings who feel insecure and under stress is the urge to hang with our own kind. And the world's greatest challenge is defining the terms of our interdependence."

In previous posts, I have written about several of these concepts, but Cohen's article put all the ideas together in a cogent and concise way. I wrote about the need for harmonious inclusion in the *Consciousness Solution*. I wrote about Piketty's book on Capitalism is my post on *Inequality*. And I wrote about how people react to anxiety and stress in *Positivity*. This post deals with interdependence, the desired outcome of inclusiveness, consciousness, and positivity.

Interdependence simply means actively seeking ways to help each other succeed. The conditions for interdependence are collaboration, trust, and respect. When people think and relate interdependently, social capital increases . . . . and also the potential for broader peace and prosperity.

We hear a lot about our interdependent web of existence. We share this planet with 7 billion people and millions of species. Due to our competitive nature and our overarching inclination for independence, we are quickly eliminating vulnerable species like the polar bear. The logical extension of these trends is that we end up eliminating ourselves.

Here is a scale to measure how we relate to each other:

5: Interdependently
4: Collaboratively
3: Independently
2: Competitively
1: Dependently

Dependent people rely on others for direction, innovation, and income. Contrary to Republican propaganda, less than 1% of the federal budget goes to welfare. Dependency almost always results in a lose-lose relationship. The dependent person loses the satisfaction of self-sufficiency and the person on whom they depend loses time and resources.

Human history can be characterized as a competitive scrambling for scarce resources. Wild animals compete for food. Greedy humans compete for power, position, and property. Highly trained athletes compete for glory and dominance. Unfortunately, our two bad genes – ego and aggression – continue to raise their ugly heads.

The United States was built on the fierce fight for independence. Ayn Rand, of course, wrote volumes on the need to pull ourselves up by our own bootstraps. Sadly, many people not only bought that idea, but failed to recognize that no one has made it "on their own." The privileged among us all had help in one form or another. At best, independent thinking and relating can result in win-win outcomes, i.e. you get what you want and I get what I want. Each person achieves his or her individual goals.

We have recently recognized that collaboration offers many benefits that go beyond individual goal achievement. People who collaborate are open to sharing and see the value in striving for the collective good. As the "team" succeeds, so also does the individual. As every country becomes more participative, productive, peaceful, and prosperous, the global economy grows.

Interdependence goes beyond collaboration because it is more active. Interdependence means having a mission beyond yourself. The purpose of interdependence is to be helpful. It is not driven by ego, greed, or aggression.

The polar bears are at risk because we have failed as a society to think and relate interdependently. We even refuse to collaborate when both parties gain from open sharing. If we continue to see the world through a competitive and independent lens, our demise won't be far behind that of the polar bear. As Bill Clinton stated, "the world's greatest challenge is defining the terms of our interdependence."

Symptoms and Systems

It's easy to see the glaring symptoms of a problem and miss the underlying systems that caused the problem in the first place.

Lets take the recent shooting of a black teenager by a police officer in Ferguson, Missouri as an example. If we look at the situation as an individual problem, we could focus on Michael Brown, Darren Wilson, or Robert McCulloch. Michael Brown was clearly the victim who didn't deserve to be shot. He was also not a saint. He was caught on video stealing from a store and then pushing the owner. When confronted by Officer Wilson, he assaulted the officer in the car, ran away, and then turned and started back at the officer. Darren Wilson was no saint either. He was probably scared, angry, and influenced by a racist culture. While technically acting within his legal rights, he did not have to resort to lethal violence on an unarmed teen-ager. Perhaps the most egregious offender, however, was Robert McCulloch, the prosecuting attorney. Not only was he clearly biased in favor of the police, but he also waited until dark fall before announcing the Grand Jury decision. One has to suspect that this action was a set-up: Prolong the investigation to stir up resentment, announce the decision at night-fall, and then point the finger at black looters and arsonists who couldn't contain their anger – thus creating the belief in some peoples' minds that the response of the black community justified Officer Wilson's actions. To me, that is sick manipulation.

However flawed each individual was in this case, the analysis of individual behavior misses the larger point. This was an eruption of an unjust, unfair system with multiple components and interactive parts. There is no question that the black community has been stuck with the short end of the stick (or the blunt end of a night stick as the case may be) educationally, economically, socially, and politically. The facts are too glaring to ignore: black kids are 21 times more likely to be killed by police than white kids; blacks are stopped, frisked, and incarcerated far more often than any other race; and most black kids grow up in under-performing, segregated schools in poor communities that are oppressively policed by white officers. Is there any doubt why rage is simmering below the surface? Until we address the systems causing that rage, we can expect the pot to boil over whenever an incident heats up the water.

Fergusen or New York, or Baltimore, or LA, or Cleveland, however, are just examples of symptoms getting more attention than systems. We need to focus less on episodes and more on conditions. We need to focus more on culture than individual behavior. This is true whether we are talking about race relations, democracy, or health care.

Yes, our democratic process is clearly broken. Any system that can re-elect George W. Bush is broken. Any system that can elect Tea Party candidates is doomed to disaster. Again, we could focus on the individual attributes of any given politician. More importantly, we need to look at how re-districting, campaign finance, and voter suppression create the conditions for dysfunctional government.

Health care is another example where there is more attention on symptoms than causes. Too many Americans are obese, stressed out, and largely sedentary. As a result, whole industries have been formed around weight control, stress management, and exercise. Unfortunately, no matter how effective these new businesses may be, they are still simply treating the symptoms of dysfunctional systems. One must ask the question, "why are people overweight in the first place?" One reason is that the food industry is dominated by high-fat, processed food grown with toxic fertilizers, pesticides and antibiotics which is then promoted by the fast food merchandisers luring children to unhealthy food. And, why are people so stressed out? One reason is that people go to work in sterile, stifling, and high stress environments many of which are dominated by toxic leaders. We could choose to focus on the health of individuals as they attempt to navigate unhealthy systems, or we could look at the systems that are making people sick in the first place.

These are just a few examples that make the point that we need to shift our focus from symptoms to systems. There is no shortage of systems to address: education, economic, political, social, health care, organizational, etc. Instead of blaming the victims and chasing the symptoms, let's start changing the systems. As Martin Luther King said, "riots are the language of the unheard."

Harmonious Inclusion

I recently visited the Brooklyn Museum to see an exhibit by Judith Scott. It was an amazing exhibition that displayed the chronology and complexity of Ms. Scott's work with innovative sculptures, unique designs, diverse materials, and beautifully blended colors. What made it even more remarkable was her biography. Judith Scott was born deaf with Down's Syndrome. At age 7, she was placed in a state institution and remained there until the age of 42. Her exclusion from society for 35 years left her essentially comatose. Her twin sister, after a powerful vision at a meditation retreat, removed Judith from the institution and brought her home. She enrolled Judith in a program called Creative Growth, a supportive environment for people with disabilities. Creative Growth treated all of their day students as artists and gave them materials to create whatever moved them. After a slow and halting start, Judith found her groove. Over her 20 years at Creative Growth, she created an abundant portfolio that is now being exhibited in some of the most prestigious art museums in the country. It strikes me that her life and her work exemplify the power of harmonious inclusion.

I tell this story because it demonstrates more poignantly than any words I could write the differences between exclusivity and inclusivity. Exclusivity alienates, diminishes, and wastes precious talent. Inclusivity activates energies, sparks passion, and leverages unique gifts. Instead of benefitting from harmonious inclusion, we are suffering from cacophonous exclusion.

Why cant' we get this right? History is an inglorious record of discordant exclusivity. For a graphic depiction of this phenomenon as it applies to our African American brothers and sisters, watch the movies *12 Years a Slave* or *Selma*. For a deeper understanding of how other immigrant groups have been abused and excluded from opportunities, check out these books:

Italians: *Elizabeth Street*, Laurie Fabiano
Irish: *Pnin*, Vlaimir Nabokov
Bohemians: *My Antonia*, Willa Cather
Jews: *Call it Sleep*, Henry Roth
Latin Americans: *The Brief Wondrous Life of Oscar Wao*, Junot Diaz
Indians: *Namesake*, Jhumpa Lahiri

If one takes even a moment to reflect upon the tremendous contributions these ethnic groups have made, it seems ridiculous that we aren't being more proactive about weaving diverse talent into our social fabric and seeking out ways to be more inclusive.

On a positive note, there now appears to be a movement toward Inclusive Capitalism. On May 27, 2014, over 220 leaders from the worlds of business and finance gathered in London to discuss the future of capitalism and how we can act to make our economic system more equitable, more sustainable, and more inclusive. While this is a hopeful sign, all the words and commitments that came out of that conference will be for naught without an elevation of consciousness. Change begins with a new level of consciousness; it doesn't end there. In our current state, inclusive capitalism is an oxymoron. Capitalism is about maximizing privatized interests whereas inclusiveness is about maximizing community well-being. Capitalism is competitive; inclusiveness is collaborative and interdependent.

Over 30 years ago, Robert Carkhuff laid out the foundations and framework of a new, inclusive capitalism. In his model, documented extensively in over 50 books, the new capitalism is more than the accumulation of financial capital; it is the development of information capital, human capital, organizational capital, marketplace capital, community capital, and cultural capital. These are the real elements of an inclusive capitalism. I still hope, at some point, the business and financial leaders of the world will turn to the real substance of inclusive capitalism instead of making flowery speeches with no models, maps, or processes to advance the idea and without a new consciousness to make it possible.

The importance of harmonious inclusion also applies to our personal lives, for example, are we open to new ways of looking at life that may disrupt our armored ideology? In her book *Love 2.0*, Barbara Fredrickson urges us to see love as a series of warm connections that are not confined to rigid and traditional paradigms. We could also open up to new methods for developing our spirituality. In his soon to be published book, *The Genius School,* Dr. Artie Egendorf describes 12 moves for activating and aligning creative energy. We need to ask ourselves how we can open up to growing physically, emotionally, intellectually, and spiritually – even though it may be disruptive and require effort to achieve harmony.

The Pulitzer Prize winning play, *Disgraced*, brilliantly portrays the difficulties we all encounter when we confront conflicting views of ourselves and others as well as how we integrate new ways of experiencing the world in the light of past history and baggage. In this case, a Muslim lawyer in a Jewish law firm attempts to deny his history and traditions, but is forced to confront different points of view with his white wife, his black law partner, his Jewish friend, and – most powerfully, with himself. The play presents in sharp relief the problem of defining who we are and how we reconcile and integrate our historical roots with our current realities and possibilities.

The challenge is more about the harmony than the inclusion. It's one thing to support a pluralistic society, and another thing to integrate religious extremists into the community. It's one thing to invite everyone to play their instruments at the same time, and another thing to make melodious music together. It's one thing to open your borders to all comers, and another thing to ensure that everyone wins. It's one thing to open our minds and hearts to new ways of relating, thinking, and being, and another thing to deal with internal conflicts and cognitive dissonance. There is a reason why most of us want to continue to do things the same old way and to operate within the bell curve. Dealing with other people at both ends of the curve is difficult. And personally, removing ourselves from our comfort zones creates tension.

The only way to change ourselves, our societies, and our world is to open up to new possibilities. The story of Judith Scott is a stark but inspiring reminder of what can happen when differences are valued and leveraged instead of exploited and abused. The play *Disgraced* reminds us that harmony can be a fleeting moment. I still think it's possible to create new harmonies and possibilities by welcoming differences into our lives. Just as musical instruments require regular tuning to make sure the sounds they produce are harmonious, so also do we need to fine-tune our instruments as we welcome new experiences into our lives.

Abuse

A final indicator of social health is the absence of abuse. As long as we are seeing abuse in any sector of our society, it is sick. Sexual slavery has never been more ubiquitous and drug abuse is still rampant, but the news media is so transfixed on the transgressions of celebrities that systemic issues remain largely unnoticed in privileged bubbles.

Yes, we are hearing a lot of sordid stories these days about professional athletes abusing their spouses and children. As horrific and wrong as these cases are, they make us think that abuse is mostly physical and is contained within a small sub-section of the population. To me, abuse is more than physical, and it is practically universal. Let me explain.

Abuse can be physical, emotional, intellectual, or spiritual. It can occur in blatant and obvious ways, or it can be much more subtle and less easily detected. Abuse can be a sin of commission or a sin of omission.

The media focuses almost entirely on the commission of physical acts of violence, e.g punching your girlfriend in the elevator and dragging her out in the hall or whipping your kid with a branch and inflicting wounds on the legs, arms and back. But physical abuse can also be less obvious. What about the abuse children feel when they are never hugged, kissed, or held tightly? Or, even on a more subtle basis, when no one attends to them by leaning in, getting on their level, looking them in the eye, and putting away all other distractions? I would say it's abusive not to attend to and hold a child enough that they feel loved, not just tolerated.

I rarely get though a day without seeing signs of emotional abuse. Again, the sins of commission are more obvious. A mother yells at her child. A spouse gives a condescending glance at his or her partner. A boss wallows in negative emotion or creates a hostile or toxic work environment. Children are told that big girls don't cry or big boys shouldn't be scared. But what about the sins of omission? For example, kids who grow up not believing that their feelings and values are understood because no one took the time to listen or respond to what they were saying. Or a child feels abandoned and neglected because they are left largely on their own – even if that means watching TV, playing video games, or surfing the internet. Not growing up in a supportive, nurturing, and loving environment seems like abuse to me.

We can also be abused intellectually. When kids are told they are stupid, doesn't this constitute abuse? When a boss dismisses an idea or puts down a suggestion, that seems like abuse to me. If employees are never asked what they think, that omission also seems abusive. What about parents who never have the time to read to their kids or demonstrate interest in their passions, aspirations, dreams, activities, or hobbies - doesn't that fall in the category of abuse? I'm not suggesting that abuse is always intentional. I get it that parents working two jobs trying to make ends meet simply run out of gas at the end of the day – or even start out with an empty tank given the cumulative stress they carry with them from the previous day, week, month, year, decade or century. I guess on a larger scale, our whole economic system could be seen as abusive.

Finally, it seems to be that one of the most abusive practices across the world, affecting billions of people, is the imposition of religious ideology on children, or adults for that matter. Whether it's the Catholics imposing chastity on its priests, or the Muslim extremists training children to kill "apostates," or Orthodox Jews not letting women pray at the entire Wailing Wall, these abuses cause spiritual malaise. In my mind, sexual oppression, dogmatic ideology, and fanatical jihad are all forms of spiritual abuse. Clearly, they are not promoting peace and compassion in the world. If you believe that evil is limiting good, then insisting on literal translations of spiritual texts or denying exposure to multiple possibilities that may not be consistent with your creed or cultural bias seems abusive to me.

My point of this riff is that we should probably resist the temptation to feel righteous because we haven't punched anybody in the face recently. Abuse is rampant, can come in many forms, and can manifest as a commission or omission. I would venture to guess that we all have not only experienced abuse at one level or another in our lives, and probably could be accused of being abusive to another – whether it's to a spouse, a child, a neighbor, or someone from another religion or culture. I can certainly claim to being abused (although I feel lucky and grateful that I have suffered so little), and I can own being abusive due to my ego, arrogance, or just simple meanness. We need to turn toward these abuses, tune into the feelings we carry, read the hurt that people feel, care about others and ourselves, and grow into kinder, gentler persons. Perhaps then, we will be better able to reach out to and join with others to create more peaceful moments if not a more peaceful world. And maybe we will find the courage to share with others our own experiences of abuse and speak out when we see abuse in any form – physically, emotionally, intellectually, or spiritually. Hopefully, we will then be able to experience the glow of peace instead of the horror of violence.

Wellness

This final chapter explores the individual possibilities that would be more easily accessible to us if we worked in healthy organizations for effective leaders in an inclusive and equitable society. Individual wellness is practically impossible for people who lack education, work in unhealthy organizations for toxic leaders, and live in a society in which success is rigged at birth. Individual wellness is the outcome of sound education, energizing organizations, inspiring leaders, and a just society under conditions of equal opportunity.

The chapter starts with a brief history of wellness and then explores the on-going possibilities of every moment at every age. It goes on to explore the importance of impartial objectivity and being able to consciously witness our physical, emotional, intellectual, and spiritual functioning. The post on Holism discusses how the parts of a whole are in intimate interconnection, such that they cannot exist independently of the whole or cannot be understood without reference to the whole, i.e. the whole is more than the sum of its parts. The chapter concludes with a summary of research that shows the benefits of positivity, serenity and intensity in our lives.

A Brief History of Wellness

In 1978, when wellness was still a strange term that few people understood, I was hired to direct one of the first hospital based health promotion/wellness programs in the country. Samaritan Health Service (SHS), the largest hospital system in Arizona, started this innovative program because health care costs were escalating and consuming a continuously increasing percentage of GDP. The Center for Disease Control had just completed a study showing that over 50% of morbidity and mortality could be attributed to lifestyle related behaviors, but only 3% of health care spending went to prevention. SHS founded Lifewise to increase its focus on prevention, address the health care cost issue, and establish itself as the leader in comprehensive health care management. Now, wellness facilities are ubiquitous and the word has become part of our common parlance. Smart-watches are even being sold to monitor our exercise and nutritional habits. The following graph shows the results of this movement.

	1978	**2014**
Total Health Care Costs	$200 Billion	$3 Trillion
Percentage of GDP	8%	18%
Percentage of health care spending allocated to prevention	3%	8%
Percentage of disease and premature death attributable to lifestyle related behaviors	>50%	>50%

What does this chart tell us? In the last 36 years, health care costs have increased 15x, spending on health care as a percentage of GDP has more than doubled, and spending on preventive health services/wellness has increased significantly. **For this enormous investment in health care, there has been absolutely no impact on our health, our behaviors, or disease prevention.** Clearly, many individuals have become much healthier as a result of many of these programs, but for the population as a whole, obesity has increased, stress has increased, and our health care system – the most expensive in the world - ranks very low compared with other countries on indicators such as infant mortality. Affordable health care represents a step in the right direction, but Republicans are doing their best to snatch defeat from the jaws of victory.

What happened?

Basically, when we think of health promotion we need to take into account not only individual health, but also organizational health. Yes, there are more marathon runners, tri-athletes, vegetarians, and people who get massages and go to Yoga classes; but unfortunately, most organizations are still soul-sucking, health-depleting places with toxic managers and abusive working conditions. And the American culture of greed and gluttony doesn't exactly support positive health practices. Income inequality has exacerbated the stress. While the top 1% can afford their health clubs, massage therapists, and high performance gadgetry, the lower 90% not only find it harder to make ends meet, but also to find affordable fresh fruits and vegetables in their neighborhood markets. It may be that wellness will turn out to be one more perk for the privileged.

What can be done to re-draw this rather dismal picture?

First, individual health and wellness needs to be seen as more than physical fitness. Second, we need to create environments that support positive health practice and well-being. I believe there are four critical organizational health areas that require different approaches: purpose, context, content, and process.

Step One: Change the PURPOSE of wellness from bicep building to performance improvement.

A recent Harvard study on "Why We Hate Work" suggests that the way we're working isn't working. Even if you're lucky enough to have a job, you're probably not very excited to get to the office in the morning, you don't feel much appreciated while you're there, you find it difficult to get your most important work accomplished, amid all the distractions, and you don't believe that what you're doing makes much of a difference anyway. By the time you get home, you're pretty much running on empty, and yet still answering emails until you fall asleep. For most of us, in short, work is a depleting, dispiriting experience, and in some obvious ways, it's getting worse.

Employees are vastly more satisfied and productive, it turns out, when four of their core needs are met: physical, through opportunities to regularly renew and recharge at work; emotional, by feeling valued and appreciated for their contributions; mental, when they have the opportunity to focus in an absorbed way on their most important tasks and define when and where they get their work done; and spiritual, by doing more of what they do best and enjoy most, and by feeling connected to a higher purpose at work.

The more effectively leaders and organizations support employees in meeting these core needs, the more likely the employees are to experience engagement, loyalty, job satisfaction and positive energy at work, and the lower their perceived levels of stress. According to the Harvard study, when employees have one need met, compared with none, all of their performance variables improve. The more needs met, the more positive the impact.

Put simply, the way people feel at work profoundly influences how they perform. What the study revealed is just how much impact organizations can have when they meet each of the four core needs of their employees.

Renewal: Employees who take a break every 90 minutes report a 30 percent higher level of focus than those who take no breaks or just one during the day. They also report a nearly 50 percent greater capacity to think creatively and a 46 percent higher level of health and well-being. The more hours people work beyond 40 — and the more continuously they work — the worse they feel, and the less engaged they become. By contrast, feeling encouraged by one's supervisor to take breaks increases by nearly 100 percent people's likelihood to stay with any given company, and also doubles their sense of health and well-being.

Value: Feeling cared for by one's supervisor has a more significant impact on people's sense of trust and safety than any other behavior by a leader. Employees who say they have more supportive supervisors are 1.3 times as likely to stay with the organization and are 67 percent more engaged.

Focus: Only 20 percent of respondents said they were able to focus on one task at a time at work, but those who could were 50 percent more engaged. Similarly, only one-third of respondents said they were able to effectively prioritize their tasks, but those who did were 1.6 times better able to focus on one thing at a time.

<u>Purpose</u>: Employees who derive meaning and significance from their work were more than three times as likely to stay with their organizations — the highest single impact of any variable in the survey. These employees also reported 1.7 times higher job satisfaction and they were 1.4 times more engaged at work.

Step 2: Change the CONTEXT of wellness from the gym to the work environment i.e. from reducing medical risk factors to improving the norms and values of the workplace.

In 1982, AT&T hired me as a consultant to design a culture-based wellness program for its one million employees. At the time, Total Life Concept was the first corporate wellness program that focused on creating a healthier work environment. Even though we didn't have the benefit of the Harvard study cited above, the program concentrated on renewal, value, focus, and purpose. The timing was fortuitous. We implemented this program just before the divestiture of Ma Bell into seven regional operating companies, many of which have now merged. The purpose of the program was to help employees manage change during one of the most tumultuous upheavals in corporate history.

Step 3: Broaden the CONTENT to include health enhancement as well as risk reduction.

In 2003, based on the work at Samaritan Health Service, AT&T, and many other clients, Barry Cohen and I published *The Complete Guide to Wellness*. This book includes 7 chapters on risk reduction and 9 chapters on health enhancement as well as a Lifestyle Possibilities Assessment. Here are the 16 areas:

Risk Reduction:

- Stop Smoking
- Weight Control
- Cholesterol Reduction
- Blood Pressure Control
- Stress Management
- Present Moment Thinking
- Low Back Care

Health Enhancement

- Fitness
- Nutrition
- Interpersonal Communication
- Self Esteem
- Managing Change
- Creative Thinking
- Job Satisfaction
- Healthy Home
- Connectedness

As you can see, there are chapters addressing the physical, emotional, intellectual and spiritual dimensions of wellness.

Step 4: Use the 5D PROCESS to implement the wellness program.

With a clear purpose (performance improvement), the right focus (cultural norms and values), and the right content (lifestyle possibilities), the last step is to use a systematic process to implement the program. For the past 30 years, we have used the 5D process to achieve significant results: Design, Diagnosis, Development, Delivery, and Determination. In 2001, Julie Meek and I published the book *Spiritual Leadership* in which we documented the process and profiled "Soul Models" who had successfully implemented 5D. Here is a brief definition of each D:

- *Design*: Creating the vision and possibilities for the future
- *Diagnosis*: Identifying solutions required to achieve the vision and the challenges that need to be addressed
- *Development*: Creating the programs and processes required to implement the solutions
- *Delivery*: Implementing the solutions
- *Determination*: Evaluating the results

With comprehensive content and a systematic process, the chances of achieving high level wellness are greatly enhanced.

The purposes of this post are to shed light on the history and evolution of wellness in America, to suggest some ideas for improving the impact of our health care and wellness spending, and to stimulate thinking on what it would take to make it easy for people to answer the question, Why I Love My Job?" When we are able to pass that simple test, we may be on the right road to wellness.

Development or Deterioration

As I begin my eighth decade, I'm challenged by the daunting task of maintaining a vital, healthy, life and continuing to grow and develop. I'm sure the first thought that crosses peoples' minds when they meet me now is, "he's old!!" That would be ok, but most people associate aging more with accelerated deterioration than continuing development. The important issue, however, is not what other people think but what we think about ourselves. Do we wake up each morning and say, "I'm old – ugh!" Or do we say to ourselves each day, "This is the day I have been given, may I rejoice and be glad in it!"

I'm not denying the relentless and inevitable toll of time. I'm simply suggesting that if we think about each moment as a new opportunity, it is more likely that new opportunities will emerge, independent of age. Why not ride the growth curve as long as we can?

There is no end point for development. Growth does not end at age 50, 60, 70, or 80. It may take a different form or shape, but it doesn't need to end. As we age, we may lose some analytical capabilities and memory speed, but other avenues open up. Howard Gardner's work on multiple intelligences applies to elderly adults as well as it does to elementary children. While our mathematical prowess may diminish after 30, hopefully our aesthetic appreciation and wisdom increases as we age.

The biggest risk as we grow older is premature cognitive commitment. In Ellen Langer's classic book on *Mindfulness,* she discusses the results of extensive research indicating that our beliefs about what happens as we age have a significant influence on our health and longevity. If we believe that old people become tired, cranky, slow, dull, and incapacitated, then we are likely to meet that expectation. If we commit early to an age = deterioration formula, that's probably what will happen to us. We can reduce that risk by re-framing our experience of aging and re-committing to growth.

The keys to continuous development as we age are decision making, responsibility, openness, adaptability, positivity, intellectual curiosity, control, social engagement and support. Langer's work demonstrates profoundly the differences between people who feel like they have some control in their lives, are able to make decisions affecting their lives, take responsibility for their care, remain open to alternative possibilities, and continue to be curious compared to those people who have no control, take no responsibility, etc. The latter group becomes dependent and acquires learned helplessness. This state leads quickly to deterioration and death. The former group strives and thrives until the very end . . . . and lives longer and better.

We need to be open to alternatives and new ways of thinking and relating, focus on process vs. outcome, play with context and perspective, and bypass old categories, habits, and routines. Our choice is simple. We can take a reactive approach to the challenges we face and shrink into a deteriorated state; or we can take a proactive approach to what's possible and continue to generate creative energy.

Most research on healthy aging addresses physical risk factors such as high blood pressure, alcohol abuse, smoking, sedentary living, and obesity. While physical health is a foundational factor in healthy aging; emotional, intellectual, and spiritual factors are also developmentally important.

Physical development is a function of activity and exercise. Emotional development is a function of social engagement, positivity, and adaptability. Intellectual development is a function of curiosity and intense mindful activity. Einstein once said, "I have no special talents, I just have a passionate curiosity." Spiritual development is a function of purpose, meditation, and mindfulness.

One positive aspect of aging is that we are less distracted and driven by urges. Our competitive instincts are less charged. Our metabolism slows down. Our primal instincts are easier to manage. As I get older, I'm finding more and more benefits to slowing down. The nick name of Rapid Rick was well grounded in observations of my impulsiveness, speed, and impatience. As I continue to practice qigong and Energy's Way, I'm learning the benefits of a less frenzied pace. Hopefully, I will continue to discover the mysteries of mindfulness and new possibilities as I begin this journey of the 8th decade.

Getting distance on our problems

Everyone has issues. They could be physical. They could be mental. They could be emotional. Or they could be a mix of all three. Some are minor annoyances. Some are major trauma. The challenge is to get enough distance on them, so we don't get lost in them or identify with them. Our bodies may not work the way we would like them to work . . . . . but we are not our bodies. Our minds might not function at the level we would like them to function . . . . . . but we are not our minds. Our emotional state may be darker than we would like it to be . . . . . but we are not our feelings. We are simply human beings trying to develop enough consciousness to be able to observe how our bodies are working, how are minds are functioning, and how are emotions are manifesting without identifying with them or imagining we are somehow free from them.

Physically, we may have diabetes, but our body is strong and athletic. Mentally, we may not have the type of intelligence that would enable us to be a neurosurgeon, but we may have an aesthetic intelligence that enables us to create or appreciate art. Emotionally, we may be anxious or depressed, but we may be sensitive interpersonally. Being able to observe and accept whatever conditions our genetic programming produced, gives us a sense of space to create who we are: our essential selves, our crystallized "I," our soul, or state of consciousness. We can't get distance on our problems if we get lost in them or identify with them by saying, for example, I am a diabetic, or I am a surgeon, or I am depressed and anxious. Getting distance means being able to say, "I am a conscious being housed in a body that is diabetic, equipped with an analytical and logical mind, and hard-wired to experience depression and anxiety." Creating a space to observe our issues gives our essential self a chance to accept the physical, emotional, or intellectual challenges we face, and still continue the work and effort of growth and development. We need to avoid being victimized by "things," and be energized by the process of living, learning, and working.

Gurdjieff uses the analogy of a horse and carriage to help us get a handle on this phenomenological process. The carriage represents our physical center, the horse represents our emotional center, and the driver represents our intellectual center. So where is our conscious being? That's the big question. Our conscious being is usually asleep or absent. Thus, the driver, horse, and carriage react to whatever situations they encounter and go about their business independent of any degree of consciousness. They simply engage in conditioned responses at a fairly unconscious, automatic, habitual level. Sometimes the carriage breaks down and needs to be fixed. Sometimes the driver gets drunk and runs the carriage off the road. Sometimes the horse gets frisky, refuses to listen to the driver, and pulls the carriage and driver into a ditch. You never know which one is going to influence the path on which they travel. And, sometimes, a conscious being wakes up in the carriage, observes what is going on, and gets all three components acting in joyful harmony.

Unfortunately, "you" never know which "being" is going to wake up in the carriage or at what level of consciousness. The "soul" in the cab could just be a visitor for a day who wants to go to Florida. The next day another being could show up who wants to go to India. On a third day, still another being could show up with a whole different idea of where to direct the driver, horse, and carriage. This being could wake up with a fighting mind, an acquiring mind, or a complying mind. Or, a dynamic being could wake up with a loving heart, an inclusive spirit, or an enlightened purpose. Over time, the goal is to have a fully-awake being occupy the carriage with a high level of consciousness.

Getting distance on our problems means being able to observe our physical, emotional, and intellectual centers without getting lost in them or over-identifying with them. For most of us, one center tends to dominate the other two centers and ignores whatever level of consciousness exists in the cabin. Some of us are intellectually driven and see emotions as weakness. Others are physically driven and totally identify with their physical prowess. Still others are emotionally driven and cling to sentimental views of the world independent of any evidence that could shake their beliefs. Some of us are more balanced than others. A few are even unified so that the physical, emotional, and intellectual centers actually work in concert and produce great music. Rare individuals achieve a level of consciousness that enables them to impartially observe how each center functions and are able to create a joyful harmony among the centers. Hopefully, we can all get enough distance on our problems to experience a few perfect moments before one of our centers raises its ugly head and takes us off our path.

Holism

Holism is the theory that parts of a whole are in intimate interconnection, such that they cannot exist independently of the whole or cannot be understood without reference to the whole, i.e. the whole is more than the sum of its parts. If you believe in the power of synergy, then 2+2 may equal 5. While it is sometimes very useful from a scientific point of view to break things down into smaller and smaller parts to analyze and measure them, what we sometimes forget is that things are lost in the breaking down and things end up missing in the re-construction. The question is, how do the parts relate to the whole?

Scientists and philosophers have pondered this question for hundreds of years. Darwin (1809-1882) said, "In order to be an astute observer, you have to be an active integrator." Kurt Goldstein (1878-1965) believed, "You can't treat a symptom without understanding the whole of the individual." In short, no empirical data can ever be readily intelligible unless grasped from an ideational frame of reference. Husserl (1859-1938) asked us to "challenge the assumption that our human experience is a mere chaotic jumble of disconnected elements." He suggested that life and soul emerge from physical material but grow into forces of their own and, in turn, influence the physical. Even earlier, Hegel (1770-1831) argued that "individual objects exist as manifestations of indivisible substance-universals, which cannot be reduced to a set of properties or attributes; he therefore holds that the object should be treated as an ontologically primary whole." He insisted that "the unity we find in our experience of the world is not constructed by us out of a plurality of intuitions." Alfred Adler (1870-1937) believed that the individual (an integrated whole expressed through a self-consistent unity of thinking, feeling, and action), must be understood within the larger wholes of society, from the groups to which he belongs, to the larger whole of mankind. The recognition of our social embeddedness and the need for developing an interest in the welfare of others, as well as a respect for nature, is at the heart of Adler's philosophy of living and principles of psychotherapy.

So what does all this mean for our contemporary lives and the daunting challenges we face?

On an individual level, it means that we can't entirely understand the emotional, spiritual, and intellectual dimensions of our lives by reducing our body parts to smaller and smaller areas of specialization. We are more than the sum of our individual body parts. As I discussed in the post on "THIS and that," it is impossible to explain every aspect of our experience. The mystery is in the experience.

On a religious level, it means we can't understand the fullness and limitations of Islam, Christianity, Judaism, Buddhism, Hinduism, etc. by assigning characteristics to the whole by the action of any one of its parts. For example, we can't understand Islam through the actions of extremist terrorist groups, and we can't understand Christianity through the actions of a few predatory priests.

On a social level, we need to distinguish between our independent desires and our interdependent needs. As Adler said, we need to see ourselves as part of the whole of humankind. We are one small part of an interconnected and interdependent fabric. The shift from independent thinking (only concerned with satisfying our personal goals) to interdependent thinking (actively seeking ways to help each other succeed) is a huge leap. The problem in achieving the shift is, as Carkhuff has suggested, we can't understand the higher in terms of the lower. As I discussed on my post, "The Consciousness Solution", if our consciousness is at the survival or tribal compliance level (levels 1 and 2), then we can't understand the requirements or benefits of harmonious inclusion or enlightened service (levels 6 and 7). All we see are enemies with whom to compete instead of partners with whom to collaborate.

Given all this background, I still believe 2 + 2 = 5, maybe even 10. I wish I could figure out a way to change the math. To me, the whole is more that the sum of the parts. I can't explain it, but I can experience it.

Positivity

In Shirzad Chamine's book, *Positive Intelligence*, he refers to Sages, Saboteurs, and PQ or positive intelligence. It's a fascinating entreaty on the battle between our higher and lower selves and posits that PQ is the tipping force in winning the battle.

It should be noted, though, that the ideas of Sage and Saboteur have been elucidated very substantively, in other terms, by others. Chamine suggests that a sage needs to empathize, explore, innovate, navigate, and activate. These are all viable steps crafted in an easy to understand format. If you look at the work of Robert Carkhuff, however, one of the most referenced social scientists of the last century, you will see that all of these concepts have been operationalized in a systematic, interpersonal and intrapersonal schematic. The Carkhuff model, first developed and extensively researched in the 60s, is as follows:

Attend	Respond	Personalize	Initiate
Interest	Exploration	Understanding	Action

As the helper attends, responds, personalizes, and initiates; the helpee, correspondingly, becomes interested, explores, understands, and takes action. The responding skills demonstrate how to be **empathic**. The model shows how to help yourself and others **explore** where you are and where you want and need to be. The skills of personalizing, and the helpee effect of understanding, bring into play the need to **innovate and navigate**. The initiative skills lead to action for yourself or for others and represent what Chamine would say is **activation**. The Sage is able to do all of these skills well with deeply steeped experience and expertise

Chamine also lists the ten saboteurs that can undermine our Sage intentions and lower our level of consciousness. Again, the origins of these ideas have been thoroughly researched in the past. In the 1940s, Gurdjieff brought tremendous wisdom to the East with the introduction of the enneagram. The enneagream is a personality test with 9 personality types and 7 levels of health within each type. Chamine's 10 saboteurs can be linked to the 9 enneagram types particularly at the lower levels of health. If you Google enneagram LEVELS OF HEALTH, these are nicely laid out. The chart below illustrates the direct comparison of the 10 Saboteurs to the 9 personality types. The Sage and the Saboteurs are imbedded in the levels of health. In my mind, the enneagram gives far greater depth and meaning to Chamine's construct, but he never mentions the enneagram in his book. It's another example of trivializing, privatizing, and commercializing a larger idea. What's really striking is that Chamine lists his saboteurs in exactly the same order as the enneagram's nine types but makes no reference to the earlier work. This correlation seems to be more than coincidence.

Chamine's Saboteurs	Enneagram Type	Enneagram Sage	Enneagram Saboteur
Stickler (Perfectionist)	1	Wise Realist, Principled Teacher	Judgmental, Intolerant Perfectionist

Pleaser (Rescuer)	2	Caring Altruist, Nurturing Helper	Self Important Saint, Exploitative Opportunist
Hyper Achiever (Competitive Performer)	3	Authentic and Self Assured Achiever	Self Promoting Narcissist, Exploitative Opportunist
Victim (Attention and Affection Seeker)	4	Inspired Creator, Self aware and self revealing Seeker	Self Indulgent Exceptionalist, Alienated Depressive
Hyper-Rational (Rational Processing – Private)	5	Pioneering Visionary, Focused Innovator	Provocative Cynic, Isolated Nihilist
Hyper-Vigilant (Always anxious)	6	Valiant Hero, Engaging Friend, Committed worker	Authoritarian Rebel, Overreacting Dependent
Restless (Seeking greater excitement)	7	Ecstatic Appreciator, Free-Spirited Optimist	Excessive Materialist, Impulsive Escapist
Controller (Need to take charge)	8	Magnanimous Giver, Constructive Leader	Confrontational Adversary, Ruthless Outlaw
Avoider Focused on positive and pleasant)	9	Self Possessed Guide, Supportive Peacemaker	Resigned Fatalist, Denying Doormat
Judge (Always finding fault with self and others)			

In the book, *Beyond the PIG and the APE*, Krisna Pendyala commercializes this idea to an even simpler level by providing clever acronyms to explain two saboteurs both of which happen to operate primarily with unhealthy Type 7s. He uses PIG as an acronym for Pursuit of Instant Gratification and APE as an acronym for Avoiding Painful Experience. The Pig and the Ape are both potential saboteurs whom we need to be able to identify and let go before they drag us into lower levels of consciousness and unhappiness.

The PQ story is a little more current and is based on recent scientific research demonstrating the phenomenon of neuroplasticity and the recent discoveries about the brain. In short, what fires, wires. The key to increasing PQ is awareness. It's impossible to make the choice to operate from your sage consciousness is you are unaware of the saboteurs that drag you down to a lower level. According to Chamine, the "Judge" rules the survivor brain which fuels your saboteurs. With high PQ, you can free your Sage to use its productive powers. You raise your PQ by practicing awareness and "self-remembering."

There are many practical exercises that can help you increase your awareness. Just starting at the very basic level, you can boost your awareness by paying attention to sensations in different parts of your body. Rub your fingers together. Wiggle your toes. Listen for your heartbeat. Scan your body for points of tension. Meditate.

Due Quach, founder of Calm Clarity, teaches specific skills for increasing resiliency and for shifting into parts of the brain that trigger positivity. For a full explanation of her story, the science behind her methodology, and the specific applications go to www.calmclarity.com.

So what's the point? Both Chamine and Pendyala have written clever, commercial books to help us more deeply understand how we operate at different levels of health and how we can use awareness and positivity to increase our performance and well-being. While they have made significant contributions to making these ideas more readable and accessible, they fall short on two counts. One, there is scant reference to the substantive body of research that underlies their theories. And, two, they give the false impression that increases in happiness and performance can easily occur if we are more aware of the animal/saboteurs who are dragging us down, and if we practice some simple exercises. It's my belief that the scholars who proceeded us deserve more credit for the work they have done, and that real change requires more effort. New science-based methodologies, such as Energy's Way and Calm Clarity, offer specific skills for achieving higher positivity, performance, and peace.

Serenity AND Intensity

There have been a plethora of articles on the independent health effects of meditation and vigorous exercise, but a dearth on the synergistic effects of combining them. In this post, I suggest that maximum effects can be obtained by bracketing or breaking up your day with an hour of intense physical exertion and an hour of complete serenity realized through deep contemplation or meditation. I am offering myself as an N of 1 for this study, but I'm hoping that, after you read the research, you will join me in this effort to optimize your possibilities.

Therapeutic interventions that incorporate training in mindfulness meditation have become increasingly popular, but to date little is known about neural mechanisms associated with these interventions. Mindfulness-Based Stress Reduction (MBSR), one of the most widely used mindfulness training programs, has been reported to produce positive effects on psychological well-being and to ameliorate symptoms of a number of disorders. The results suggest that participation in MBSR is associated with changes in gray matter concentration in brain regions involved in learning and memory processes, emotion regulation, self-referential processing, and perspective taking.

In a practical application of this research, as reported in the New York Times, Mark T. Bertolini, the 58-year-old chief executive of Aetna, the health insurer, was sitting in his Hartford office wearing a dark suit and a crisp, white, French-cuffed shirt. But instead of a necktie, he wore a shiny metal amulet engraved with the Sanskrit characters "sohum."

Roughly translated, sohum means "I am that," and repeating the phrase is used to help control breathing in meditation. Mr. Bertolini says the word also signifies a divine connection with the universe. (He has a similar design tattooed on his back.)

In recent years, following a near-death experience, Mr. Bertolini set about overhauling his own health regimen, as well as reshaping the culture of Aetna with a series of eyebrow-raising moves. He has offered free yoga and meditation classes to Aetna employees; more than 13,000 workers have participated. Aetna says participants show increased productivity, and report less stress and pain.

As a result of his commitment to health and fairness, Bertolini has transformed a stodgy insurance company into one of the most progressive actors in corporate America. Aetna's stock has increased threefold since Mr. Bertolini took over as chief executive in 2010, and recently hit a record high. It's a decidedly groovy moment for the company, and Mr. Bertolini is reveling in his role as an idealistic, unconventional corporate chieftain.

More than one-quarter of the company's work force of 50,000 has participated in at least one class, and those who have report, on average, a 28 percent reduction in their stress levels, a 20 percent improvement in sleep quality and a 19 percent reduction in pain. They also become more effective on the job, gaining an average of 62 minutes per week of productivity each, which Aetna estimates is worth $3,000 per employee per year. Demand for the programs continues to rise; every class is overbooked.

I could site numerous other examples of the effects on productivity and performance from mindfulness training. For example, Due Quach, the founder of Calm Clarity (www.calmclarity.org) has demonstrated improvements in resilience, purpose, and positive emotions as well as reductions in peak stress levels, frequency of toxic stress, and negative emotions.

Independently, there is also a large body of research that shows the effects of exercise on health. One of the most fascinating studies was conducted in Finland with identical twins that enabled the researchers to eliminate potentially confounding genetic and environmental variables.

As reported in the New York Times, it turned out that these genetically identical twins looked surprisingly different beneath the skin and skull. The sedentary twins had lower endurance capacities, higher body fat percentages, and signs of insulin resistance, signaling the onset of metabolic problems. (Interestingly, the twins tended to have very similar diets, whatever their workout routines, so food choices were unlikely to have contributed to health differences.)

The twins' brains also were unalike. The active twins had significantly more grey matter than the sedentary twins, especially in areas of the brain involved in motor control and coordination.

Presumably, all of these differences in the young men's bodies and brains had developed during their few, brief years of divergent workouts, underscoring how rapidly and robustly exercising — or not — can affect health, said Dr. Urho Kujala, a professor of sports and exercise medicine at the University of Jyvaskyla who oversaw the study. Dr. Kujala said he believes that the results strongly imply that the differences in the twin's exercise habits caused the differences in their bodies.

More subtly, the findings also point out that genetics and environment "do not have to be" destiny when it comes to exercise habits. For these particular twins, whether their genes and childhoods nudged them toward exercising regularly or slumping on the couch, one of the pair overcame that legacy and did the opposite (for better and worse).

In addition to the physical benefits of exercise, both short-term exercise and long-term aerobic exercise training are associated with improvements in various indexes of psychological functioning. Cross-sectional studies reveal that, compared with sedentary individuals, active persons are more likely to be better adjusted, to perform better on tests of cognitive functioning, to exhibit reduced cardiovascular responses to stress, and to report fewer symptoms of anxiety and depression. Exercise training reduces depression in healthy older men and in persons with cardiac disease or major depression. Exercise also improves self-confidence and self-esteem, attenuates cardiovascular and neural responses to mental stress, and reduces some type A behaviors. Although exercise training generally has not been found to improve cognitive performance, short bouts of exercise may have short-term facilitative effects. Vigorous, high-intensity exercise appears to boost the results.

Regardless of the variation of methods used to report exercise intensities, a consistent pattern appeared with the findings. All of the epidemiology studies that have controlled for energy expenditure found greater cardio-protective benefits from the higher aerobic exercise intensities as compared to the moderate aerobic exercise intensities. As a matter of fact, no epidemiological study has reported a greater cardio-protective benefit from moderate intensity versus vigorous aerobic exercise. The clinical studies showed very similar results. When energy expenditure was controlled for in the study, the vigorous exercise intensity was more beneficial in altering one or more risk factors to coronary heart disease. Specifically, in relation to the coronary heart disease, the #1 cause of mortality in America, aerobic exercise of a more vigorous type resulted in lower incidences.

So it's fairly safe to say that the independent effects of meditation and vigorous exercise are profound. The question is, what would happen if we combined them, i.e. an hour per day of serenity and an hour per day of intensity?

For the last 20 years, I have maintained a disciplined routine of incorporating serenity and intensity in my life. I lift weights three times per week at the local gym and walk 5-10 miles per day. In addition, I practice meditation, qigong, and Energy's Way (www.energysway.com) everyday. Yes, I have missed days and weeks, but not many.

On February 11, 2015, I turned 70. To celebrate, my wife and I spent two weeks hiking in Patagonia. We were able to walk up to 14 miles per day on very challenging trails in the Andes. I returned feeling energized and calm. I acknowledge that I am very lucky to have the time and resources to exercise, meditate, and travel as much as I do. I also know that if I didn't include these disciplines in my life, I would have a much harder time managing my ADHD, ODD, OCD, and Tourette Syndrome. I not only have the motivation to incorporate serenity and intensity in my life, I also have the need, the skills, and the support – all of the elements of successful change programs.

If you are a researcher, I encourage you to conduct a double blind, randomized control trial on the synergistic effects of meditation and vigorous exercise. If you are just trying to muddle your way through the stresses and challenges of everyday life, I encourage you to include more serenity and intensity in your life.

Conclusions

In conclusion, I hope you found this book as intoxicating as a blended whiskey and as refined as an aging wine. The riffs and rants were meant to be an open sharing and genuine caring for our tenuous lives on the planet earth. Our lives are over-flowing with possibilities if we can reach the right perspective. I sincerely hope these perspectives elevate your possibilities.

References

Note: I am including these references so the reader can do further investigation if desired. Most of these authors have multiple works that could have been cited and are worth exploring further. For example, according to World Cat, Robert Carkhuff, whom I reference multiple times in this book, has 231 works in 611 publications, in 9 languages and 25,177 library holdings. I am just indicating the name of the author and one selected book to facilitate the search for more information.

Adams, Jane. Twenty Years at Hull House.
Adler, Alfred. Superiority and Social Interest.
Anthony, William. Psychiatric Rehabilitation.
Armstrong, Karen. The Case for God.
Aslan, Reza. Zealot.
Aspy, David. Toward a Technology for Humanizing Education.
Banks, C. The Essential Rumi.
Bechler, J. Physics of Consciousness.
Bell, J. S. Speakable and Unspeakable in Quantum Mechanics.
Benson, Herbert. The Relaxation Response.
Boch-Mobius, Imke. Qigong meets Quantum Mechanics.

Bohm, David. The Undivided Universe.

Borysenko, Joan. Minding the Body, Mending the Mind.

Capra, Fritzof. The Tao of Physics.

Carkhuff, R. R. The Science of Possibilities.

Carroll, James. Christ Actually.

Carroll, Sean. The Particle at the End of the Universe.

Cather, Willa. My Antonia.

Chamine Shirzad. Positive Intelligence

Chopra, Deepak and Mlodinow, Leonard. Where Science and Spirituality Meet.

Darwin, Charles. On The Origins of Species.

DeBroglia. Louis. Certitudes and Incertitudes of Science.

Diaz, Junot. The Brief Wondrous Life of Oscar Wao,

Dye, Thomas. Power and Society.

Eagleman, David. Incognito: The Secret Lives of the Brain.

Egendorf, Artie. Genius School.

Epstein, Greg. Good without God.

Espenshade, Thomas, and Chang Chung. The Opportunity Cost of Admission

Fabiano, Laurie. Elizabeth Street.

Frankl, Victor. Man's Search for Meaning.

Frederickson, Barbara. Love 2.0.

Gardner, Howard. The Theory of Multiple Intelligences.

Gerber, Vibrational Medicine.

Goethe, Hohann Wolfgang. Faust.

Golden, Daniel. The Price of Admission.

Goldstein, Kurt. The Organism.

Goldstein, Dana. Teacher Wars.

Gurdjieff, G. I. Beelzebub's Tales to His Grandson: All and Everything.

Harris, Sam. Waking Up.

Hawking, Stephen. Grand Design.

Hegel, Georg Wilhelm Friedrich. Phenomenology of Spirit.

Husserl, Edmund. Logical Investigations.

Isaacson, Walter. Profiles in Leadership.

Kabat-Zinn, Jon. Wherever You Go, There You Are.

Kafka, Franz. The Trial.

Koch, Christof. Consciousness: Confessions of a Romantic Reductionist.

Kunitz, Stanley. The Collected Poems of Stanley Kunitz.

Lahiri, Jhumpa. Namesake.

Langer, Ellen. Mindfulness.

Lao Tzu. Tao te Ching.

Lencioni, Patrick. The Five Dysfunctions of a Team.

Moore, Thomas. A Religion of One's Own.

Mukunda, Gautam. Indispensible: When Leaders Really Matter.

Nagel, Thomas. Mind and Cosmos.

Nietzsche, Frederich. Beyond Good and Evil.

Pagels, Elaine. The Gnostic Gospels.

Pendyala, Krisna. Beyond the PIG and the APE.

Piketty, Thomas. Capital,

Planck, Max. Eight Lectures on Theoretical Physics.

Pnin, Vlaimir Nabokov Bohemians.

Radin, Dean. Supernormal.

Roth, Henry. Call it Sleep.

Ryle, Gilbert. The Concept of Mind.

Sandberg Sheryl. Lean In.

Schwartz, Tony. The Power of Full Engagement.

Storr, Anthony. Churchill's Black Dog, Kafka's Mice.

Tich Nhat Hanh. Peace is Every Step.

Tononi, Giulio. Phi, A Voyage from the Brain to the Soul.

Wilber, Ken. Spectrum of Consciousness.

Wittgenstein, Ludwig. Philosophical Investigations.

Wright, Robert. The Evolution of God.

Zigarmi, Pat. Leading at a Higher Level.

Acknowledgments

First and foremost, I want to express my love and appreciation for my two amazing daughters who contributed significantly to this book, but more importantly, give my life meaning in so many ways. Rebecca encouraged me to start a blog which led to the creation of this book. Emily and her significant other, Danny Scales, provided invaluable feedback and created the front and back cover.

I also want to thank my many mentors along the way: in particular, Bob Carkhuff and Barry Cohen who were invaluable sources for broadening and deepening my perspectives and expanding my possibilities.

Clearly, this book could have never been written without the help and support of so many friends and colleagues with whom I have worked over the years, especially: Orlan Boston, Dottie Brienza, Dario Benedetti, Russ Campanello, Matt Cohen, Neil Dhar, Peter Fasolo, James Fieger, Mary Alice Fox, Ron Irwin, Jesse Marmon, Molly McCauley, Julie Meek, Chris Newell, Bill O'Brien, Due Quach, Michael Serino, Gary Stauffer, Cinny Streidl, Bob Weller, Lisa Zigarmi and

Pat Zigarmi, who read the posts when they were fresh off the press and gave me helpful feedback and the encouragement to continue. Thank you!!

Finally, a special thanks to my Vietnam buddy and interdependent friend, Artie Egendorf, who not only provided the most immediate responses and suggestions for each post, but also stimulated the deepest dialogue and reflection about how to write with more openness and clarity. Please check him out at www.energysway.com. What he is developing is true genius.

About the Author

Richard (Rick) Bellingham has over 30 years of experience as an organizational psychologist in executive coaching, strategic planning, organizational learning, and leadership development. He has consulted with over 200 organizations worldwide at the C-suite level. Rick has worked with executives in over half of the Fortune 100 companies during the course of his career.

Rick is the CEO of iobility, a New Jersey based consulting group, and has been an adjunct faculty member at Harvard University where he co-founded the Forum for Intelligent Organizations. In addition, he has taught culture change, healthcare management, and leadership development at several universities.

Rick has held executive positions within corporate settings including SVP of Human Resources at Parametric Technology, and VP of Organizational Learning at Genzyme, Additionally, he has provided pro-bono services at the Board level for the past 25 years for organizations including the YMCA, Visiting Nurses Association, and Homeless Solutions.

As a consultant, Rick has provided executive coaching feedback, training, and leadership development in companies ranging from small businesses to large multi-nationals. Rick has worked extensively in Asia, Europe and Latin America. He has published numerous articles in peer-reviewed publications and has written 15 books on leadership, culture, and HR strategy. Some of his books include The Leadership Lexicon, Ethical Leadership, Leadership Myths and Realities, HR Optimization, Corporate Culture Change, and Virtual Teams. Rick holds an Ed.D. in Counseling Psychology.

Printed in the United States
By Bookmasters